D1164610

W O R K - U P S

For nearly a year, Sailors have known they will soon depart for a six-month deployment to the other side of the world, far from family and friends, to help keep the peace and protect America's interests. Maybe they will see some "action" and fire shots in anger. Maybe it will be quiet in that far corner of the globe. What's certain is that they will come home changed in ways they can little anticipate as they complete their work-up and ready to deploy.

They train on the ship, hard, with a purpose, to become the best, conducting numerous exercises during short periods underway away from home. And they prepare at home for the extended separation from the comfortable world of family life. Deploying means that ten-hour workdays will be stretched longer. But they know that real-world ops provide the unique ingredient that makes the life of a Surface Warrior challenging and rewarding.

The difficulty of explaining this to a Navy wife or husband who will stay at home, or to friends who labor in an "eight-to-five" civilian world, can be frustrating. How can you express the serenity of sailing on a dark ocean thousands of miles from land and watching shooting stars streak across the horizon in a perfectly pitch black sky? How do you convey the excitement and satisfaction of leading a group of young people, sharing your life's experiences to help them become more than they are today and to serve their country with honor and pride? How do you put into words the dread of facing an angry sea that crashes against the hull of your ship...with little more than a few inches of steel between you and oblivion? How do you articulate that serving America at sea is a privilege, a challenge, and a thrill that can not be replicated anywhere?

So, we labor to bring voice to deep, almost subliminal emotions, to communicate what cannot be fully fathomed by anyone who does not share the special fellowship of the Surface Warrior.

And, we know that the sooner we start preparing our families, the better the six months of absence will be weathered by us all. We tell them as much as possible about what we will do, where we're going, and how we'll keep in touch. But most of all, we try to keep the family close in a time when it is natural to want to draw apart, to build walls, to look away.

Many families — young and old — go through turmoil during this period we call "work up." They argue more frequently, as if instinct tells them to separate emotionally from each other as one way to make the deployment date less difficult. Those who "stay in" ultimately will discover that closeness is a state of mind that remains undiminished by great distance.

As we look to compelling personal needs, there are hundreds of other preparations that must be made. Most are accomplished during the last month before we sail, a period reserved for less onerous work schedules and leave from shipboard duties. We tackle a seemingly unending list of household projects that need to be completed, car repairs and periodic maintenance that will ensure safe transportation for the coming months, archiving phone numbers and directions to all the places that may be unfamiliar, and preparing powers of attorney and wills to provide security for the family if....

And there are the days that we set aside to take family outings and build memories that will have to last for 180 days. These days are sacred. They are for family.

Finally, the departure day arrives, as if a juggernaut that cannot be turned away. The family piles into the car and drives together to the pier. It is usually a quiet ride. There are not many words that seem appropriate. Sometimes small talk checks the nerves and fills the silence ever so briefly. Tears well up in the eyes of husband and wife as they think about how much they will miss each other. In a city of several million people or a ship of 300 souls, they will each soon feel very much alone. They will sleep in empty beds — one always too small and the other suddenly too large.

There are few words that can assuage the chill of finality, as the family is about to tear apart with the six lines that hold the ship to the pier. Young children know that Mom or Dad will be gone for a long time, but they really have no idea what that will mean to "family." Parents know, and they cry for their children.

The car finds its way to the parking area and rolls to a stop among so many similar cars and people looking away. Very few Sailors talk among themselves as they head toward the ship that will be their home for the next half-year; many make rapid departures with a short glance back to make the farewell a quick one. Some of us prefer to embrace intensely the moment, somehow hoping we can have both worlds — the one that lays ahead and the one we'll leave behind — at the same time.

Then we must go.

We kiss our children and give them a big hug as tears well up in our eyes. The littlest ones still have no clue about what it is all about; but they now become scared at the unknown and begin to cry. Mom and Dad — husband and wife — kiss; they hold each other so fiercely that nothing can come between them. We say goodbye.

From the brow of the ship, we turn and wave at the car and family, and then we vanish from their sight. The journey — the adventure — begins...again.

Lieutenant Commander George S. Capen, U.S. Navy

Riders of

"Any man

who may be asked

in this century

what he did

to make

his life worthwhile...

can respond with

a good deal of pride

and satisfaction,

'I served

in the

United States Navy'."

PRESIDENT JOHN F. KENNEDY

the Storm

Riders of the Storm

A PHOTOGRAPHIC TRIBUTE TO AMERICA'S SURFACE WARRIORS

By Brian R. Wolff

Introduction by:
RADM Michael G. Mullen, USN,
Director, Surface Warfare Division

Foreword and text editing by:
Scott C. Truver, Ph.D.

Cover: USS HAYLER (DD-997) slices through heavy seas on maneuvers. The last ship of the highly successful SPRUANCE (DD-963)-class general-purpose destroyers, HAYLER was originally ordered in 1979 as a new-design "DDH" — reflecting the Congress' intent to increase the helicopter-carrying capability of the class. As built, however, DD-997 is a "straight-stick" SPRUANCE. Powered by four LM-2500 gas turbine engines, HAYLER can reach top speeds well in excess of 30 knots. The ship, like all other SPRUANCES, was designed and built around anti-submarine warfare as its primary mission area, reflecting the need to counter the Cold War Soviet submarine fleet. However, it also carries NATO Sea Sparrow anti air warfare missiles and has been modified with the Mk-41 Vertical Launching System, allowing Hayler to launch long-range Tomahawk Land-Attack Cruise Missiles (TLAMs), which makes the ship an important element of the 21st century Navy.

PAGE 1: For centuries Sailors have been going to sea while loved ones stay behind. The initial sadness and shock of seeing a loved one sail off, possibly into harm's way, for six months has never changed, even though the modern-day sailor has e-mail and satellite phones to stay in touch.

TITLE PAGE: The old escorts in the young as USS DALGHREN (DDG-43) rides the waves in the North Atlantic side by side with USS YORKTOWN (CG-48) on their way to an exercise in Norway. This was a great storm for photography but not such a smooth ride for the embarked Surface Warriors. With more accurate weather-reporting techniques and gas turbine engines, most modern combatants are able to steer around storms rather than ride the storms out. Still, to "go in harm's way" sometimes means having to take on the beautiful savagery of an angry sea.

ABOVE: "Red sky at night, Sailors' delight...red sky at morning, Sailors take warning." Standing watch at sunrise on board USS HAYLER (DD-997), one of the delights of a seagoing life that America's Surface Warriors enjoy, knowing they are helping to keep the peace in a still-dangerous world.

PAGE 6-7: A U.S. Navy Beach Detachment Sailor hustles out of the way of the blast from an air cushion landing craft (LCAC) during Exercise Kernel Blitz, at Camp Pendleton, California, north of San Diego. The Kernel Blitz exercises, recently teamed with the Navy's Maritime Battle Experiment, pave the way for innovative tactics, techniques and procedures with today's — and tomorrow's — equipment.

Published by International Intellectual Property Inc. (IIPI), Brian R. Wolff, President
Photographs © Brian R. Wolff / IIPI, ALL RIGHTS RESERVED
Foreword © Scott C Truver, Ph.D., ALL RIGHTS RESERVED
Remainder of text © IIPI, ALL RIGHTS RESERVED

Photo editor Joanne Donnelly Seglem
Compiled and edited by, Brian R. Wolff, Joanne Donnelly Seglem and Scott C. Truver, Ph.D.
Jacket Design by Brian R. Wolff & Joanne Donnelly Seglem
Designed by Carl Berkowitz and Danielle Tengelics Bodolosky
Illustration Page 150-151, United Defense
Page 152-153, Integraph

©International Intellectual Property Inc. 2000
All Rights Reserved
No part of this book may be reproduced in any form, except brief excerpts for the purpose of review, without written permission of the publisher.

Riders of the Storm
ISBN:0-9671097-0-1
Library of Congress Catalog No 00-103228
First Printing, 2000
Printed in China

Any Inquiries should be directed to the publisher at :

IIPI
321 Richard Rd. Yardley, PA. 19067 , USA
Tel 215-428-0817, Fax 215-428-0819
E mail iipi@aol.com , www.iipinet.com
www.fromtheseabooks.com

TABLE OF CONTENTS

Riders of

Rear Admiral Michael G. Mullen, U.S. Navy

For centuries, the magnificence and vastness of the sea has lured adventurous Sailors to explore its seemingly endless horizon. Beautiful yet mystifying, it offers one day a memorable sunrise and starlit night, and the next terrifying seas and howling wind.

We, the mariners of today, learned just like our heroes of old that despite new ship designs and advanced technologies, the sea still commands our deepest respect and constant vigilance. It cannot be subjugated, only admired. This beautiful book fittingly captures the sea's indomitable spirit and is a tribute to the Sailors who have made it their livelihood to share in its grandeur.

I discovered at an early age the thrills of life at sea. I recall watching with awe as a junior officer the ship's bow slice through whitecaps, the green flash at sunset, the starlit skies during a midwatch, and experiencing the excitement of pulling into an overseas port for the first time. As a Battlegroup Commander some twenty-five years later, I still enjoyed these timeless pleasures and the continuity of a Sailor's life. The same pleasure Admiral Dewey enjoyed from the flying bridge as he watched USS OLYMPIA's bow cut through the waters of Manila Bay, en route to one of the Navy's greatest victories, is enjoyed today as Sailors stand the watch around the globe; the same star-filled sky Admiral Kinkaid gazed at as he awaited Admiral Nishimura's Southern Forces at the decisive Battle of Surigao Strait; the same feeling the crews of Commodore Perry's Black Ships undoubtedly felt entering Shimoda Harbor, ending Japan's period of isolationism — these moments, and many more left unspoken, become our rich reward for answering the call of the sea. They are part of our proud heritage, binding us together as Surface Warriors.

Our maritime dominance is founded on forward-deployed U.S. Naval forces, whose presence deters potential aggressors from testing our nation's resolve.

the Storm

Surface ships remain the backbone of this engagement strategy. A highly visible emblem of America's power, a ship-of-the-line is our first line of defense against potential hostile forces forward, projecting American power worldwide with the ability to affect events ashore. In a typical year, surface forces participate in over 100 major exercises with over 50 countries and make over 3,000 port visits all over the world.

Through exercises and port visits, the Navy and Marine Corps serve as ambassadors, strengthening U.S. ties with allies and establishing new relationships and partnerships. From war winning to peacekeeping, to maritime interception operations and evacuation operations, these Sailors have seen it all; they've "been there and done that." In the words of the Commanding Officer of USS CARNEY (DDG 64), we bring "505 feet of American fighting steel to any fray throughout the world."

However, to make a ship a warship requires highly trained, dedicated Sailors. There are many professions and careers found at sea, both old and new. From a Quartermaster who still practices the ancient art of shooting stars daily to the highly skilled fire controlman maintaining sophisticated radars, the quality of our Sailors makes us a great Surface Navy. These Sailors are given tremendous duties and responsibilities at a young age, unmatched in any other profession. From the eighteen year-old Helmsman maintaining a ship 140 feet alongside an oiler for over an hour to the Petty Officer with his finger on the trigger to the ship's missiles, they stand the watch.

These Sailors are all volunteers and their sacrifice keeps our Navy on station, combat ready throughout the oceans of the world. No other profession enjoys more respect, prestige and admiration than serving in the Armed Forces.

The vivid photos throughout "Riders of the Storm" accurately capture the spirit and enthusiasm of Surface Navy professional men and women. I hope this book inspires its readers, as it has me, to reflect with admiration at the courage, adventure, and sacrifices of our American Surface Warriors. For those of you who serve in the Surface Navy, you truly are the best America has to offer. Throughout my career as a Surface Warrior, I have been proud to serve with and humbled by the dedication, endurance and spirit of the men and women who have chosen this demanding life. I am grateful for your friendships, your Warrior Spirit and your dedication "beyond the call."

May God bless you and yours.

RADM Michael G. Mullen, USN

"I wish to have
no
connection
with any
ship
that does not
sail fast,
for I intend to
go in harm's way."

ADMIRAL JOHN PAUL JONES

Old and new. Although the most modern and sophisticated global positioning and locating systems are available, with positional accuracies in the tens of feet, it's always good to have a backup capability . . . just in case. Here a Surface Warrior on board USS Mitscher (DDG-57) uses technology hundreds of years old — a sextant — to "shoot the stars" to locate his ship on the broad ocean.

Previous Page: USS Monsoon (PC-4), on maneuvers off the coast of southern California. The Navy's Cyclone (PC-1)-class patrol craft are configured for coastal warfare and special operations with Navy Sea-Air Land (SEAL) forces, as well as the spec-ops troops of the other Services. Although a commissioned Navy warship, with a lieutenant serving as Commanding Officer — operationally these craft come under the control of the Commander, U.S. Special Operations Command. Manned by four officers and 24 enlisted personnel, in addition to a platoon of spec-ops forces in dedicated berthing, and armed with a variety of effective weapons, the PCs have proven extremely valuable in maritime interdiction operations in the Mediterranean and counter-drug ops with the U.S. Coast Guard in the Caribbean.

The Commanding Officer of USS MITSCHER (DDG-57), at right, surveys the local and regional situation in the Adriatic Sea during the Kosovo crisis, 1998-1999. The days of the captain having to be on the bridge to fight his — or her! — warship are all-but over, as today sophisticated intelligence "pipes" linking naval and national sources, data-fusion systems, and large-screen displays in CIC — Combat Information Center — provide more accurate and timely information than ever before possible — critical elements in gaining an all-important "Knowledge Advantage" over America's adversaries.

The five-inch gun on USS Arleigh Burke (DDG-51), as the warship steams home during sunset, provides one element of the warship's main battery. It is effective against other surface ships, some air targets and provides important twelve mile range of Naval Surface Fire Support for forces ashore. The warship's Close-In Weapon System — CIWS, a.k.a. "sea-whiz" — rapid-fire gattling gun is located just aft the five-inch weapon, forward of the bridge, and is capable of rates of fire exceeding 3,000 rounds per minute against high-speed anti-ship cruise missiles, slower aircraft and helicopters and small, agile surface targets, like Boghammer speedboats.

ABOVE: USS Arleigh Burke can operate, refuel and rearm helicopters, but cannot hangar them. Later "Flight II A" variants of the DDG-51 class have been fitted with hangars, making them capable of embarking two of the Navy's SH-60 Seahawk multipurpose helicopters.

LEFT: USS Mitscher (DDG-57) on patrol in the Adriatic during one of the many confrontations over Kosovo.

The USS Vella Gulf (CG-72) steams past USS Philippine Sea (CG-58) at right, during a turnover in the Adriatic during the Kosovo crisis. These Aegis warships are the most powerful and capable anti-air — and soon, anti-ballistic missile — warships in the world, and provide highly accurate land-attack capabilities against military and infrastructure targets.

Above: Loading canisters into USS ARLEIGH BURKE (DDG-51) Mk-41 Vertical Launching System — VLS — at Yorktown Naval Weapons Station, Yorktown, Virginia. The USS BUNKER HILL (CG-52), some TICONDEROGA (CG-47) class Aegis cruisers, all ARLEIGH BURKE (DDG-51) Aegis destroyers and several SPRUANCE (DD-963) general-purpose destroyers are fitted with the VLS. The VLS can be loaded with canisters containing SM-2 Standard Missiles, a highly effective surface-to-air missile for defending against attacking aircraft and anti-ship cruise missiles, Tomahawk Land-Attack cruise Missiles (TLAMs), and Vertical Launch ASROC (Anti-Submarine Rocket) weapons. Although some Aegis warships' VLS modules have been fitted with on-board cranes to allow underway replenishment of these weapons at sea, it has proven difficult in operation to do so. For this reason, later DDG-51s have been built without the VLS cranes, permitting another six weapons to be loaded-out compared to the earlier destroyers.

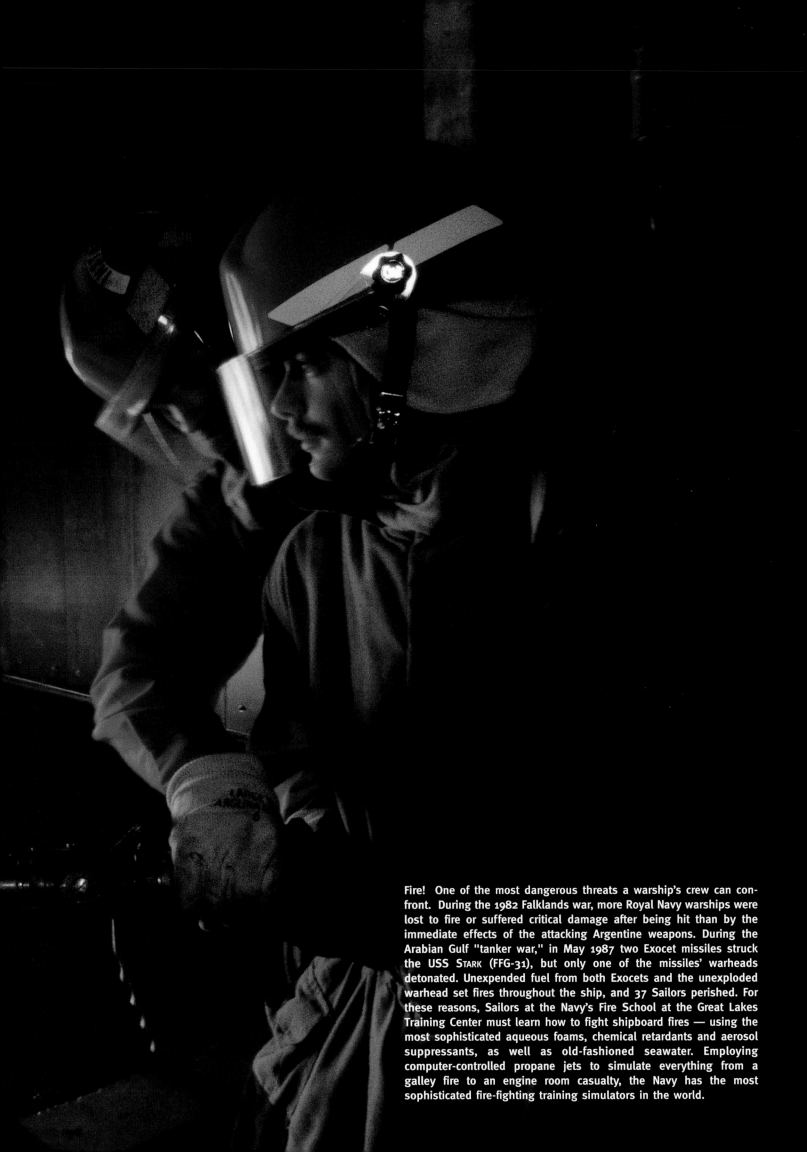

Fire! One of the most dangerous threats a warship's crew can confront. During the 1982 Falklands war, more Royal Navy warships were lost to fire or suffered critical damage after being hit than by the immediate effects of the attacking Argentine weapons. During the Arabian Gulf "tanker war," in May 1987 two Exocet missiles struck the USS STARK (FFG-31), but only one of the missiles' warheads detonated. Unexpended fuel from both Exocets and the unexploded warhead set fires throughout the ship, and 37 Sailors perished. For these reasons, Sailors at the Navy's Fire School at the Great Lakes Training Center must learn how to fight shipboard fires — using the most sophisticated aqueous foams, chemical retardants and aerosol suppressants, as well as old-fashioned seawater. Employing computer-controlled propane jets to simulate everything from a galley fire to an engine room casualty, the Navy has the most sophisticated fire-fighting training simulators in the world.

Warship.

Scott C. Truver, Ph.D.

No other word quite captures the imagination — and dread — of people who from their coastlines look out to the broad expanse of the ocean and lands far beyond the horizon. It symbolizes and manifests the essence of a nation's power to command the seas and to influence events on shore, thousands of miles from home waters. It signifies the ability to go in harm's way, to defend against invaders from the sea, to protect or hold at risk vital seaborne commerce, and to take the fight to the enemy and win.

From the earliest days of the fledgling Republic, the U.S. Navy's surface warships — men-of-war, ships-of-the-line, frigates, and sloops — and the men who sailed them have protected America and extended the Nation's reach. First to gain Independence at the great cost in lives and national treasure, then to safeguard American interests in the Mediterranean against the depredations of Barbary pirates and to open trade with the Far East, later to quell rebellion and keep the Republic intact, and later still to fight two wars to end all wars, the men and today increasingly the women — who are the heart and soul of the Navy's surface forces — have sustained and projected America's power world wide. So it has been, and will continue to be into the 21st century and beyond.

Warship.
RIDER OF THE STORM
Protector of the Nation, its citizens, interests, and friends.

The provenance of the U.S. Navy's surface forces at the advent of a new century and millennium lies with the schooner HANNA, which in September 1775, under the command of Captain Nicholson Broughton, was the first of General George Washington's makeshift fleet to take a British prize. A month later, "Washington's raggle-taggle fleet," in the words of naval historian Nathan Miller, numbered six

Sailors aboard USS PHILIPPINE SEA (CG-58) in the Adriatic prepare lines for the trip home after supporting Allied Force operations and launching Tomahawk Land-Attack Cruise Missiles against Serb targets in the spring 1999 Kosovo crisis.

vessels; in some six months of operations these ships took 38 prizes of war before they were disbanded in 1777. From this rather audacious beginning until the disaster of Pearl Harbor on 7 December 1941, not only were the U.S. Navy's surface forces the backbone of the fleet, they were the fleet and the American Sailors who commanded and crewed them helped to forge a nation from the keel up.

"I wish to have no connection with any ship that does not sail fast," declared John Paul Jones, " for I intend to go in harm's way." "We have met the enemy," Master Commandant Oliver Hazard Perry wrote in a dispatch in the afternoon of 10 September 1813, "and they are ours. Two Ships, two Brigs, one Schooner and one Sloop." "Damn the torpedoes," Admiral David Glasgow Farragut called out from the rigging of USS BROOKLYN in the early morning of 5 August 1864, during an assault on Mobile Bay, "full speed ahead!"

"You may fire when you are ready, Gridley," Commodore George Dewey ordered the captain of the cruiser USS OLYMPIA as his fleet entered Manila Bay on 1 May 1898.

"Small boys," Rear Admiral Clinton A. F. Sprague ordered his destroyer escorts as a powerful Japanese force moved through the San Bernardino Strait in the morning of 25 October 1944, "intercept!"

Prior to World War II, the surface warship was the focus of the U.S. Fleet. The nascent submarine and naval aviation/aircraft carrier forces were, in the mainstream, viewed as peripheral to the Navy's surface — especially battleship — forces, although the carriers especially made slow but steady progress in operational thinking during the 1930s. The destruction at Pearl Harbor of much of the Navy's battleship and cruiser forces in the Pacific and the rapid preeminence of naval aviation and aircraft carriers during World War II ushered in a 50-year period during which the Navy's surface forces would be considered primarily "escorts" to carrier task forces and battle groups. Throughout the post-World War II period, the large-deck aircraft carrier — not the Navy's surface warship — became the locus of U.S. general-purpose naval power and planning. Indeed, a seminal surface warship analysis in the mid-1960s underscored the key supporting role for surface warships as escorts, and throughout the Cold War surface warship force levels and mixes were more often than not justified according to the numbers and types of aircraft carriers in the Fleet.

However, since the fall of the Berlin Wall in 1989, America's Surface Warriors have been in the forefront of a revolution at sea. With the introduction of long-range surface-launched strike weapons, the invention of a robust naval theater air defense against anti-ship cruise missiles and theater ballistic missiles, and programs for futuristic stealthy warships, the Navy's surface forces are once again at the fulcrum of a renaissance in naval strategy, doctrine, tactics, and operations.

But today's innovations and experimentation in naval warfare have their legacy in the Surface Navy's near-constant embrace and pursuit of technological advantages to ensure, as President Teddy Roosevelt envisioned at the turn of the last century, a "Navy Second to None." The transition from sail to steam in the mid-1800s continues in the evolution to gas turbines in today's and electric propulsion in tomorrow's surface warships and, ultimately perhaps, what has been called the "all-electric Navy." The move from smoothbore cannon to rifled guns some 150 years ago presaged the coming of extended-range guided munitions and "fire-and-forget" land-attack weapons that are now making their way to the operating forces. The promise of "network-centric warfare" and "cooperative engagement" is founded on a history of technological innovation that saw radio replace signal flags as primary communications tools and satellites link ships in a virtual web of data, information and knowledge.

With the end of the Cold War and new strategic concepts shaping the Navy's plans, programs, and operations for littoral warfare, America's Surface Warriors and their multimission warships have once again become key elements for naval planning and operations. Some elements of the Fleet — particularly the Aegis Theater Ballistic Missile Defense cruisers — are increasingly being regarded as "strategic" assets. Although the President still asks "Where are the carriers?" at the outset of crises from the Balkans to the Arabian Gulf to the Taiwan Strait, increasingly he also wants to know where the "Tomahawk shooters" are — the multimission surface warships armed with devastatingly accurate long-range strike weapons. In broad terms, the Nation's surface forces today comprise:

• Surface Combatants — cruisers, destroyers, and frigates — take the battle to the enemy. These ships perform a variety of combat missions and tasks, including anti-air, anti-surface, anti-submarine, and land-attack operations. They are armed with guns, missiles, torpedoes, radars, sonars and other electronic sensors and countermeasures systems. In the near future, selected cruisers will also be capable of defense against theater ballistic missiles, while new concepts for DD-21 destroyers armed with hundreds of long-range, precision-guided weapons will provide regional commanders a much-enhanced land-attack and strike capability. The Navy in 2000 has been limited to a force of just 116 surface combatants — comprising TICONDEROGA (CG-47)-class guided-missile cruisers, ARLEIGH BURKE (DDG-51) guided-missile destroyers, SPURANCE (DD-963)-class destroyers, and OLIVER HAZARD PERRY (FFG-7)-class guided-missile frigates — although recent assessments have articulated the need for some 140 surface warships in the near future.

• Amphibious Warfare Ships carry and land Marines on hostile territory, using helicopters, tilt-rotor aircraft, air-cushion landing craft and amphibian assault vehicles. The Navy looks to a force structure of 36 amphibious warships that can make up 12 Amphibious Ready Groups (ARGs) consisting of WASP (LHD-1) and TARAWA (LHA-1) amphibious assault ships, HARPERS FERRY (LSD-49) and WHIDBEY ISLAND (LSD-41) landing ship docks, and the new construction SAN ANTONIO (LPD-17)-class landing platform docks.

• Mine Countermeasures Ships are specially configured to detect and neutralize or destroy naval mines, from shallow to deep-water environments. Working with the Navy's Airborne Mine Countermeasures (AMCM) helicopters and Explosive Ordnance Disposal (EOD) teams, these ships are indispensable to the Navy's ability to carry out operations in littoral areas. It is critically important to recognize that 14 of the 17 U.S. Navy ships that have suffered combat damage since the end of World War II were mine victims. Three ship types comprise the Navy's surface mine force: AVENGER (MCM-1) multi-mission ships, OSPREY (MHC-51) modular coastal minehunters and USS INCHON (MCS-12) mine countermeasures command, control and support ship.

• Command Ships provide critical command, control, communications, and intelligence systems to support forward-deployed planning and operations.

• Coastal Patrol Craft are small, fast craft capable of supporting numerous coastal combat and clandestine missions conducted by Navy Sea-Air-Land (SEAL) teams and other-service special operations forces.

Today, the Navy's Surface Warriors are being asked to do much more with much less. The major issue confronting the Navy's surface forces is the continuing high operational deployment tempos required to satisfy peacetime global commitments and crisis-response needs. These have become a serious drain on increasingly scarce resources for "recapitalizing" the surface fleet with the ships, sensors, weapons and other equipment that will ensure its ability to satisfy daunting operational commitments. Billions of dollars are needed to acquire the platforms and equipment and train the men and women who will serve America in the decades to come.

The U.S. Navy's surface forces — the core of America's naval expeditionary forces — provide the Nation with a flexible and effective

instrument of security policy with which to promote stability and project power in regions of importance to the United States. Forward-deployed, combat-credible surface forces are vitally important to shaping the global security environment and helping to assure access to overseas regions. Moreover, they enable timely and frequently the initial crisis response — anytime...anywhere — from the sea. The ability to reassure friends and allies, deter potential adversaries, and engage in combat at all levels of intensity makes America's surface warship especially valuable to the nation in peace, crisis, and war.

These ships are built to fight. And the men and women, who together stand ready to defend America and its interests, know how.

Scott C. Truver

Marine Lieutenant John Marcinek is greeted by a young girl in Gilanje, Kosovo, only minutes after the Marines secured the sector.

USS Constitution

"Old Ironsides". USS Constitution is the symbol of "The Historical U.S. Navy"...embodiment of the customs and traditions and soul that make Surface Warriors who and what they are...today and for the centuries yet to come. President George Washington and General Henry Knox knew what they needed in the six frigates that Congress authorized on 27 March 1794. As recounted by naval historian Nathan Miller, "The vessels should combine such qualities of strength, durability, swiftness of sailing, and force," General Knox wrote to Joshua Humphreys, "as to render them superior to any frigate belonging to the European powers." Constitution would meet this requirement and then some. Built of live oak — five times as durable as white oak in common use — and red cedar, with her undersides sheathed in copper armor, and longer, wider in beam, and of finer lines than any existing frigate, the three-masted Constitution was clearly "built to fight!" Rated to carry 44 guns, in practice Constitution was at times fitted with 55 weapons, including 24-pound long guns and short-barreled 32-pound carronades that were particularly deadly at close range. Constitution saw her first action against the British packet ship Sandwich on 11 May 1800, and perhaps her greatest victory against the British frigate Guerriere on 19 August 1812, which came as a great shock to Great Britain. According to historian Miller, "The Times of London" had earlier derided the small U.S. Navy as "a handful of fir-built frigates under a bit of striped bunting." For nearly two decades, the Royal Navy had emerged victorious from virtually every ship-to-ship encounter with an upstart American warship. No more.

Modern-day "Jack Tars" — able-bodied seamen — clamber about the rigging of USS CONSTITUTION in Boston Harbor. The oldest commissioned warship in the U.S. Navy, "Old Ironsides" remains heart of the Navy of Today and Tomorrow. On 21 July 1997, CONSTITUTION set sail for the first time in more than a century, as Operation Sail 200 inaugurated the ship's 200th birthday celebration. The world's oldest commissioned warship afloat sailed under her own power off the coast of Massachusetts with the same six-sail configuration that she normally used in battle. She sailed in formation with two modern U.S. Navy warships, the Aegis guided-missile destroyer USS RAMAGE (DDG-61) and the guided-missile frigate USS HALYBURTON (FFG-40). There was also a fly-over by the famed Blue Angels F/A-18 Hornets. CONSTITUTION, maintained as a national monument at Charlestown Navy Yard in Boston, had completed a four-year overhaul to restore her to original hull strength. In-depth structural tests, evaluations of the ship, and a lengthy training program for the crew prepared the ship for this historic voyage in Massachusetts Bay — the first since 1881.

Commanding Officer of USS Constitution, Commander William F. Foster, U.S. Navy, in full uniform of the day... 200 years ago, that is. In 1998-1999, controversy swirled about Constitution and plans for the ship to make an open-ocean voyage, one much more demanding on the 200-year old warship than the Operation Sail event two years earlier. More comprehensive hull surveys indicated that it would have been too dangerous to take the ship out into unsheltered waters and the plans were dropped. She was too valuable a symbol of the Nation to take the risk.

Right: A Surface Warrior salutes as the Colors are lowered on USS Constitution.

The once-great ships are now no more than a "Ghost Fleet." Here, in the Philadelphia Navy Yard, ships that once ruled the waves, wrested control of Pacific islands from their Japanese conquerors, and projected U.S. military power throughout the world during the Cold War rust away...over-grown by weeds and neglect. Indeed, the Philadelphia Navy Yard itself is a victim of the end of the Cold War and the need for "down-sizing" and "restructuring" of the Navy's shoreside "infrastructure" — lean and mean — for the battles of the 21st century.

USS Iowa (BB-61) at sunrise. Although the Navy's battleships had been the focal point of the Fleet, the disaster of Pearl Harbor changed the calculus of naval power and ushered in the age of Naval Aviation, all-but relegating the fast battleships to a carrier-escort role. With her four sisterships — New Jersey (BB-62), Missouri (BB-63), and Wisconsin (BB-64) — Iowa (BB-61) was the largest surface warship ever built in the United States, at 57,350 tons full load, and armed with 16-inch guns. Only the World War II Japanese battleships Yamato and Musashi were larger, at 70,000 tons and armed with 18.1-inch guns. Although three of the Iowas were decommissioned shortly after the end of World War II, with Missouri retained as a training ship in partial commission, both Missouri and New Jersey were activated for naval gunfire support duty during the Korean War. By 1957, all ships were once again decommissioned. New Jersey was again reactivated during 1968-1969, and during her 120-day service on the gun line off Vietnam she fired 5,888 rounds of 16-inch ammunition and 14,891 rounds of 5-inch shells.During the early years of the first Reagan Administration, all four ships again were recommissioned, with a two-phase modernization plan proposed to upgrade the ships with Vertical Launching Systems (VLS) and to allow them to operate AV-8B Harrier vertical or short takeoff or landing (V/STOL)

aircraft. (Earlier proposals during the 1950s had identified the IOWA battleships as possible platforms for Polaris ballistic missile modifications, but none was carried out as the decision was made to base the Polaris system in ballistic missile submarines.) However, funding constraints in the mid-1980s limited the ships to rather modest upgrades, including the addition of armored box launchers for the Tomahawk Land-Attack Cruise Missile. On 19 April 1989, IOWA suffered an explosion in her Number-Two 16-inch gun turret, with one officer and 46 enlisted crewmen killed. Both WISCONSIN and MISSOURI participated in Operation Desert Storm in January-February 1991; together these ships launched 52 TLAMs and fired 1,083 16-inch rounds — the last time the battleships fired their weapon in anger. MISSOURI was retained in active service with a much-reduced crew into 1992, and was present at a commemoration ceremony in Pearl Harbor on 7 December 1991, the 50th anniversary of the Japanese attack. MISSOURI was the scene of the Japanese surrender ceremony in Tokyo Bay on 2 September 1945, officially the end of

USS Dᴀʜʟɢʀᴇɴ steams the Atlantic. Designed as "destroyer leaders" in the early/mid-1950s, the Fᴀʀʀᴀɢᴜᴛ (DDG-37) class was originally planned as "all-gun" surface warships. But the increasing Soviet anti-ship cruise missile threat — launched from long-range bombers, surface warships and missile craft, and submarines — convinced the Navy to acquire these ships with the Terrier/Standard Missile system for fleet air defense. During service lives that reached into the early 1990s, Dahlgren and her nine sisterships saw the revolution at sea first hand. USS Kɪɴɢ (DDG-41) and Mᴀʜᴀɴ (DDG-42) were the test ships for the Naval Tactical Data System — NTDS — that in many respects is the progenitor of today's Network-Centric Warfare concepts and systems. Mᴀʜᴀɴ later also served as the test ship for the eight-inch Major Caliber Lightweight Gun, which, although never fielded, would have greatly increased the Surface Navy's gunfire support capabilities compared to the five-inch guns that are in the Fleet today. The need for "fires from the sea" in direct support of forces ashore has generated several important programs —upgrades to existing guns, extended-range guided munitions, high-velocity land-attack missiles — that will ensure the Surface Navy's key roles in 21st-century military strategies.

USS GEMENI (PHM-6), last of the six-ship "PEGASUS"-class PHMs — Patrol Combatants–Missile (Hydrofoil), rides on her foils at speeds greater than 40 knots. The six PHMs originally were conceived as heavily armed missile craft for sea-control operations in restricted seas, for example, in the Aegean. Armed with eight Harpoon anti-ship missiles and a rapid-fire 76-mm gun, they never committed to that role, completing their service to the nation alongside the Coast Guard in anti-drug operations in the Caribbean.

USS Iowa (BB-61) fires a broadside of nine 16-inch shells. Each 16-inch projectile, as 2,300 pounds, has been likened to "throwing a Volkswagen beetle" to ranges of 23 nautical miles. The increasing costs of ownership — during World War II service as many as 2,900 men served on the battleships, but "only" 1,500 during their 1980s' renaissance — has effectively consigned these ships to waterfront naval museums. Mid-1990's proposals for "Arsenal Ships" and the Navy's new DD-21 "Land-Attack" destroyer program have indicated the promise of leading-edge technologies to provide the much-needed, long-range striking power to support the land battle, but to do so with crews of perhaps no more than 95 people.

For America's Surface Warriors, the mission comes first. It is the only true measure of their success in peace-time, crisis, or war. This unique group of people evolved from a proud tradition that reaches back to the earliest days of the Nation's history. They are America's naval warrior elite, prepared to defend their country from dangerous threats at home and abroad.

The sea is their home. Superlative mariner skills are their core competencies. Going "in harm's way" means more than mission success in the face of a determined foe. It means the ability to navigate in heavy weather, dangerous seas, shoal water and in close company with other warships and vessels. Sailors in their hearts — Warriors in their souls.

These sailors are key to the Navy's ability to use the sophisticated and powerful weapons that are in the Fleet today and that will be introduced in the decades ahead. America demands the highest professional and personal standards, from Admiral to Seaman Recruit.

As the U.S. Naval Services look to the future, America's Surface Warriors must remain ready to conduct prompt and sustained combat operations at sea, in Combat Information Centers (CIC), on the bridges of the Navy's multi-mission warships, and throughout the chain of command across the spectrum of the Nation's needs.

ABOVE: Officers monitor air traffic in the Tactical Flag Command Center (TFCC) on board USS CORONADO. In crisis and conflict, sorting out the "good guys" from the "bad guys," and making sure the Navy keeps tabs on all other "gray" or neutral air traffic are critical needs.

UPPER LEFT: USS CORONADO (AGF-11), one of the Navy's four Fleet command ships. With these ships approaching an average age of 34 years, the requirement for effective command and control of Navy, Marine Corps, Joint and other-nations' forces in future crises and conflicts has generated calls for a future new-design Joint Command and Control Ship — JCCX.

Looking forward from the bridge of USS GEORGE PHILLIP (FFG-12), an OLIVER HAZARD PERRY (FFG-7)-class anti-submarine frigate, a P-3 Orion Maritime Patrol Aircraft crosses the bow during a multinational sub-hunting exercise with Thailand. Although the erstwhile Soviet submarine fleet is now more than a shadow of its Cold War force, this does not mean that the Navy can ignore it. During the past decade, faced with increasing political turmoil and a wrecked economy, Russia still managed to continue the modernization of its undersea forces. And, the U.S. Office of Naval Intelligence continues to warn about the third-world submarine threat, with some countries acquiring the best systems Russia and other countries have to offer, including advanced Air Independent Propulsion (AIP) submarines, submarine-launched anti-ship cruise missiles, wake-homing torpedoes, and sophisticated naval mines. The U.S. Navy and the naval forces of America's allies and friends ignore the ASW dimension at their peril.

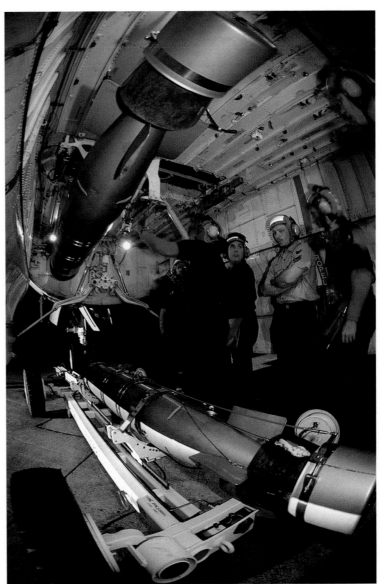

Sailors in Sigonella, Italy, load lightweight ASW torpedoes in a P-3 Orion Maritime Patrol Aircraft for duty over the Adriatic during the Kosovo crisis. Concerns about the what was left of Yugoslav submarine force kept the Navy focused on all dimensions of naval warfare in the littorals — not simply naval air sorties and TLAM strikes against Serbian targets ashore.

In a brief respite from her plane-guard duties, the Aegis guided missile cruiser USS SHILO (CG-67) departs after completing an underway replenishment — UNREP — from the nuclear-powered aircraft carrier USS CARL VINSON (CVN-70). First truly tested during World War II and refined to a near-exact science during the Cold War, the U.S. Navy's underway replenishment systems and station ships ensure that the Fleet will not be hamstrung by the need for support facilities and infrastructure ashore in some volatile region. Unlike their ground-based sister-services, the Air Force and the Army, the Navy and Marine Corps are the essence of what it means to be expeditionary — they carry their "packs" on their own "backs."

45

Chief boatswains mate takes on stores from an underway replenishment ship enroute to the Adriatic. The highlines, king-posts, and tensioning systems have been perfected by decades of trial, error, and focused engineering. No other navy even comes close to the UNREP capabilities of the U.S. Navy.

Not knowing what they will encounter, but assured in their skills and their faith, U.S. Marines —
Brothers-in-Arms --— recite the Lord's Prayer on board USS KEARSARGE (LHD-3) before going
ashore in Greece and heading, ultimately, to help keep the peace in Kosovo.

KOSOVO

Projecting Power in Land Locked Countries

The on-scene presence of forward-deployed naval forces sometimes needs to be augmented to meet emergency needs. As the political crisis in Yugoslavia deteriorated in the early spring 1999, the guided-missile cruiser USS VELLA GULF (CG-72) sprinted across the Atlantic at record speed, arriving just in time to launch cruise missile strikes in the opening phases of Operation Allied Force.

THE SIGNIFICANCE OF KOSOVO

Kosovo was probably the single greatest growth experience of my life. As we received the call to duty we did not know what to expect. We had prepared for every possible mission we could imagine. As we loaded our LCACs, we said a prayer and asked for the safety of all the Marines and Sailors going ashore. Yet, when we arrived in Kosovo, it was to a hero's welcome — certainly not what we expected!

The average American safely at home will never be able to fathom the pain and suffering that the Kosovars — both Serbs and Albanians — experienced, but the Marines were exposed to everything: intense hatred; senseless violence…the sight of blood and corpses…the smell of gunpowder and the din of fire-fights…the fear of an uncertain environment…the love and awe in a child's eyes…the sight of a military vehicle littered with thank-you flowers…the joy of helping others. We will probably never see anything like this again, but I am sure that we helped to mold a new generation by caring for and teaching the children. And I am even more convinced that we were transformed into better human beings. Our hearts swell with pride and our step is more confident. I do know that wisdom is not a function of age, but experience. Our Marines and Sailors are now much wiser. I only pray that we are able to teach others what we have learned.

Lt. John Marcinek USMC
26th Marine Expeditionary Unit

Dressed as Artie the Arctic Bear, a Sailor from the fast combat support ship USS Arctic (AOE-8) entertains sailors on board the Aegis guided-missile cruiser USS Vella Gulf (CG-72) during an UNREP that allowed the Aegis warship to make best time on her way to help resolve the Kosovo crisis.

Expeditionary Warfare...
From the Sea

To the casual observer it looks like a military "alphabet soup."In reality, this "acronym-rich" language describes the "ingredients" of a new course, an unprecedented vision for the Navy-Marine Corps Team that will soon realize a

Corps' evolving concepts of operations that in essence are a marriage between classical blue-ocean naval warfare and maneuver warfare focused on the warfighting needs of expeditionary operations in the world's littorals and extending their reach well inland. The Navy and Marine Corps continue to test and refine these concepts and to develop vital capabilities to deliver naval forces to an area of operation, to move embarked forces directly to their inland objectives, and to support them from bases at sea.

Above: A key element in the Marine Corps "mobility triad," the LCAC — "Landing Craft Air Cushion" vehicle — has delivered troops, weapons, and humanitarian relief supplies in crises from the Mediterranean, to the Arabian Gulf, and to the shores of Bangladesh.

Top Left: A Marine sits atop his armored vehicle in the well deck of the amphibious assault ship USS KEARSARGE (LHD-3), awaiting orders to move ashore to Greece and then on to Kosovo.

The OMFTS force of the near future will operate well OTH — "over the horizon" — from sea bases 50 nautical miles or more from the coast. With ranges in excess of 200 miles, they will use the sea as a "maneuvering space" to gain and sustain tactical surprise and operational advantages over any adversary.

The multi-ship ARGs — "Amphibious Ready Groups" — comprising a variety of special-purpose amphibious assault ships and dock landing ships, will rapidly deliver tailored forces directly to objectives ashore, bypassing topographic or defensive barriers. From a small, "Special Operations-Capable" Marine Expeditionary Unit, to "Marine Corps-Minus" — multi-divisional Marine Expeditionary Forces — the Navy-Marine Corps surface-maneuver force will generate a high operational tempo to frustrate and confuse an enemy's defensive and offensive operations.

The LCAC — "Landing Craft Air Cushion" vehicle — was introduced to the Fleet in 1986 and continues to spark innovations in tactics, techniques, and procedures. Riding on a cushion of air some four feet above the surface, it is capable of transporting a 75-ton payload at speeds of more than 40 knots and can "land" on 70 percent of the world's coastlines. (Traditional landing craft are limited to just 20 percent of potential landing zones.) With ranges of some 300 nautical miles at 35 knots, the LCAC provides the surface-lift backbone to a combined-arms OTH assault. It has proven to be exceptionally valuable for conducting non-combatant evacuations and humanitarian support operations in remote areas, in addition to its warfighting capabilities. In one 24-hour period during Operation Desert Storm in early 1991, for example, LCACs made 55 runs in high seas and winds, delivering critical equipment ashore to support 20,000 Marines. On their way back home in

May 1999, the LCACs proved invaluable in response to another sort of crisis. In Operation Sea Angel (May-June 1991), four of the Navy's LCACs provided critical humanitarian support to the people of Bangladesh, who had been battered by 140 mile-per-hour winds and a 20-foot tidal surge spawned by Typhoon Marian that killed 140,000. The LCACs were the only platform capable of delivering much-needed aid to isolated islands off the coast.

Poised to join the Fleet in 2001, the **MV-22** Osprey is a tilt-rotor, Vertical/Short Take-Off or Landing aircraft that will replace the Marine Corps' obsolescent CH-46E and CH-53D helicopters. The vertical-airlift backbone for future OTH operations, the MV-22 is the world's only transport aircraft capable of taking off and landing vertically and converting in-flight. Capable of airspeeds approaching 270 knots, significantly faster than the fastest helicopter, the MV-22 can transport 24 com equipped

Marines or a 10,000-pound external load, has a service ceiling of 25,000 feet, and has a self-deployment range of 2,100 nautical miles with just one in-flight refueling. The Osprey's flexibility, speed, and improved survivability greatly increase the ARG's combat power, and the MV-22 is key to future maneuver warfare success.

Left: Reality is everything. You train as if you are going to fight. During workups and exercises in the United States, Marine Corps forces call in naval fires on a Camp Pendleton beach.

Right: Maneuver from the sea and sustain movement on land, gain surprise and make decisions faster than your enemy can react to them. Marines come ashore during Kernel Blitz exercises in Camp Pendleton, honing skills that will be needed in some real-world crisis, somewhere, some day.

Marines from CAT Platoon, 26th Marine Expeditionary Unit, on the ground in Macedonia, head for Kosovo. Increasingly, the U.S. military has been committed to peace-keeping and peace-enforcement operations, sometimes under the auspices of the United Nations...sometimes unilaterally when America's interests are at risk and a multinational response cannot be lashed together. In the spring 1999, NATO countries stood behind the collective action, although coordination at the front lines, particularly following the pull-out of Serb forces from Kosovo, was at times strained.

Right: A LCAC maneuvers in the Coral Sea off of the coast of Australia.

the AAAV is a leap forward for the Naval Services and will enable the OMFTS concept to become reality.Looking to a future of information superiority and cyberspace operations, the Navy and Marine Corps recognize that they will have to put warriors ashore to ensure that national objectives can be achieved — in humanitarian crises as well as major theater wars. The Naval Services' expeditionary warfare "alphabet soup," will capitalize on emerging technologies and innovative thinking to guarantee that the Navy-Marine Corps Team will have the capabilities needed to take decisive action as an independent force, an element of a "joint" multi-service task force, and as a partner in multi-national operations.

Marine officers set up shop in the Gilanje headquarters of the Ministry of Interior Police, known by its Serb initials, "MUP." Watched over by a photograph of Yugoslavian President Slobodan Milosevic who gambled everything on NATO's inability to work together, and lost, the Marines plan for their next day of peace-enforcement in a troubled land.

Left Above: What to expect? When will the next shot be fired...this time at us? U.S. Marines in Gilanje, Kosovo, man check points and disarm KLA Members.

Left Below: A Navy doctor attached to the 26th MEU attempts unsuccessfully to administer first aid to a KLA member wounded while removing mines after cease-fire was declared by NATO.

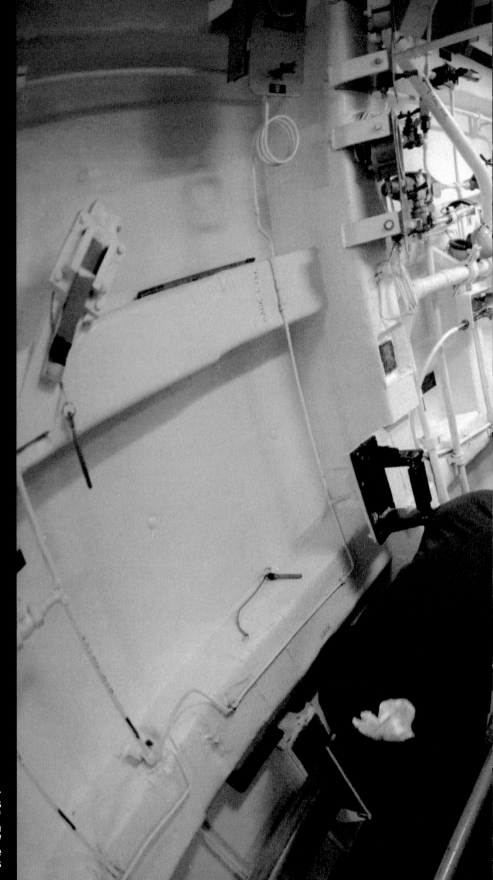

"This was

the first

crisis that

we never

fired

missiles"

Although his ship had been in the thick of cruise-missile launches in previous operations, "This was the first crisis that we never fired missiles," one Sailor declared, as he and his buddies on board the USS ANZIO(CG-68) prepared Mk 46 ASW torpedoes during the Kosovo crisis, just in case action against some unfriendly submarine was warranted.

A multimission Seahawk SH-60 helicopter lands on board Anzio after completing a patrol over the Adriatic. Although primarily an ASW platform, the Seahawk carries out anti-ship, maritime interdiction, and search and rescue duties, among other tasks that might be thrust upon its crew.

Sprinting into the Mediterranean, with the Rock of Gibraltar framed on

The new replaces the old. Modern ship-handling simulators, linked to powerful computers, can put novice and

veteran Sailors through demanding situations, including once-in-a-lifetime scenarios that task skills almost to the

breaking point. The old-style simulator in Little Creek, Virginia, is no longer used; in the best of situations it was

barely adequate for the Navy of the 20th — let alone the 21st — century.

TRAINING

As the Navy looks to the Revolution in Military Affairs to ensure it will have the technologies, systems, weapons, and equipment to meet the operational demands of the 21st century, so too individual Sailors and Marines must have the intelligence, training, and skills to carry out the daunting tasks ahead. The future calls for a highly trained, broadly educated, and razor-proficient core of individuals who come together as a cohesive team capable of performing stressing missions. The on-going revolution in Navy training is the foundation for operational excellence in the 21st century.

To meet these needs, the Navy's training infrastructure is being modernized and made more efficient to take advantage of a host of new technologies. Investments in training technologies, modeling and simulation, and a shift toward increased training in an operational setting will better support the preparation of today's Surface Warriors for the dangers they will face at sea.

Solid evidence of this revolution in training can be found at the Recruit Training Center and Damage Control (DC) "A" School at Great Lakes. The challenging "Battle Stations" training at Great Lakes is dedicated to instilling a common set of core values, overcoming mental and physical challenges, and promoting teamwork and unit cohesion. By providing a strong foundation of character, integrity, and leadership training, the Navy is building a force of innovative and resourceful individuals capable of making timely, effective decisions under pressure.

Smoke kills. When an Argentine Exocet missile struck HMS Sheffield during the 1982 Falklands War, the warhead detonation did not sink the ship. It was the inability of the crew to fight the fires that soon raged throughout the stricken warship, frustrated in their desperate damage-control efforts by a dense, acrid smoke, which caused the crew to abandon ship. "USS Buttercup" in Norfolk, Virginia, gives Sailors a full range of damage-control problems, from dense smoke to stemming the flooding in a internal compartment, experiences that may make the difference between life and death.

Train…train…and train some more. To be ready for anything that might be thrown at you. The sophisticated trainer-simulator at the Fire-Fighting School in Great Lakes, gives Sailors a taste of what they could encounter in the fleet.

"We're the best!" Top: Signalmen go through their paces and new boatswains mates get their first taste of life at the Navy's Deck Crew School at the Great Lakes Training Center.

At the Great Lakes Weapons School, technicians get hands-on training and experience with complex guided-missile launching systems,
here the Mk-26 twin-armed launcher with a dummy SM-2 surface-to-
air missile training round on the rail.

71

Page 72–75: New recruits...Next-generation Sailors ready themselves for Boot Camp, where they will be transformed from civilians to Warriors. In recent years, the Navy has had difficulty achieving it recruitment goals — missing targets by nearly 7,000 recruits in 1998. Since then, a variety of new and innovative recruiting practices have borne fruit, but some 12,000 at-sea billets were gapped in 1999 because the trained people were not at hand.

The problem...competition with a "red hot" civilian economy where jobs were plentiful and wages — particularly in "high-tech" fields — skyrocketing.

It only looks like a "boat school."

When the founders of the United States Naval Academy were looking for a suitable location, it was reported that then-Secretary of the Navy George Bancroft decided to move the Philadelphia Naval Asylum School to "the healthy and secluded" location of Annapolis in order to rescue midshipmen from "the temptations and distractions that necessarily connect with a large and populous city." The Naval School was established without federal funding, at Fort Severn, a 10-acre Army post in Annapolis, Maryland, on October 10, 1845, with a class of 50 midshipmen and seven professors. The curriculum included mathematics and navigation, gunnery and steam, chemistry, English, natural philosophy, and French. Five years later, the Naval School became the United States Naval Academy. A new curriculum went into effect requiring midshipmen to study at the Academy for four years and to train aboard ships each summer.

As the U.S. Navy grew over the years, the Academy expanded. The campus of 10 acres increased to 338. The original student body of 50 midshipmen grew to a brigade size of 4,000. Congress authorized the Naval Academy to begin awarding bachelor of science degrees in 1933. The Academy later replaced a fixed curriculum taken by all midshipmen with the present core curriculum plus 18 major fields of study, a numerous and diverse elective courses, and advanced study and research opportunities.

Since then, the development of the United States Naval Academy has reflected the history of the country. As America has changed culturally and technologically so has the Naval Academy. The Naval Academy first accepted women as midshipmen in 1976, when Congress authorized the admission of women to all of the service academies. Women comprise about 13 to 14 percent of entering plebes — or freshmen — and they pursue the same academic and professional training, as do their male classmates.

The classes now at the Naval Academy will produce many of the leaders of the Navy and Marine Corps for the next 30 years. In the course of their careers, the military and political circumstances of the world will take unexpected turns. Military force structures will change as new technology takes hold. Naval Academy graduates will meet these new challenges with courage, honor and integrity upholding cherished traditions, always leading to a new and better future.

Rites of passage. Plebes no more. At the end of their first year at the U.S. Naval Academy in Annapolis, Maryland, new third classmen strive to yank a plebe's "dixie-cup" hat from the well-greased Herndon Monument, an obelisk in front of Chapel, and replace it with an officer's hat — tradition has it that the first person to replace the hat will be the first person of the class to make admiral.

Three years later, they take the oath as a new Navy ensign or Marine Corps second lieutenant, but with much more to experience and learn and share. It's been a tough four years, but the friendships will last a lifetime and the education will allow them the foundation for success.

Officers in the computer simulation lab at the Naval War College, Newport, Rhode Island, learn to address complex, time-critical tactical scenarios. Their decision-making capabilities and skills will be stressed in the lab, so that when the time comes, they will do the right thing at sea.

A target drone from Fleet Activities in Okinawa leaves the flight deck of USS GEORGE PHILIP (FFG-12), during the CARAT 99 Exercise off the coast of Thailand. The "drone ex" gave ships from the Royal Thai Navy an opportunity for real-world target practice.

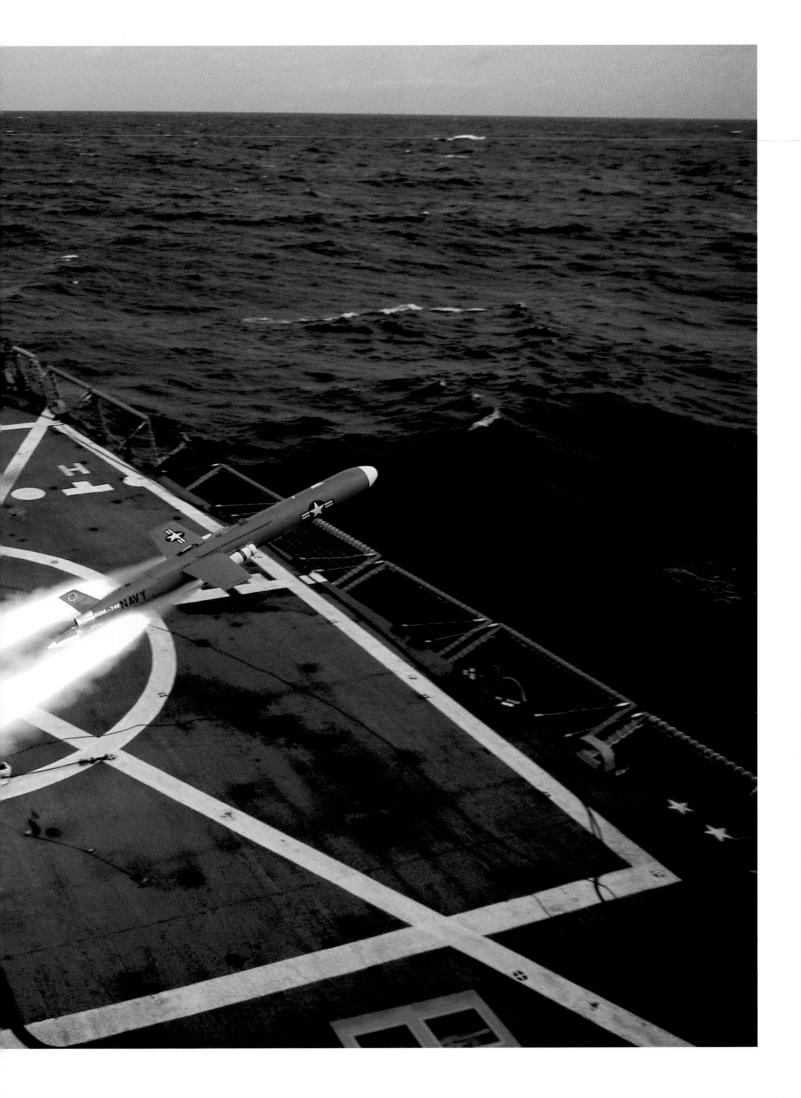

The Navy-Coast Guard relationship has almost always been strong and enduring. Since the earliest days of the new United States, from the Quasi-War with France in 1798 to Operation Desert Storm in 1991, the Coast Guard and the Navy have served side-by-side. Here, a Coast Guard SH-60J Jayhawk helicopter practices a rescue lift with USS MONSOON (PC-4), and a Coast Guard rescue swimmer leaps off MONSOON into frigid waters. These and many other interoperability skills will be even more important in the new century as the Navy and Coast Guard seek common approaches to ensuring America's national and maritime security needs are met.

Sailors on board USS VELLA GULF work on one of the ship's four main propulsion gas turbine engines. Adapted from an aircraft engine, each of VELLA GULF's LM2500 turbines generate about 25,000 shaft horsepower, and with all four on line can drive the ship at speeds in excess of 32 knots.

Built to fight! USS ARLEIGH Burke (DDG-51) launches a Tomahawk cruise missile during a "missile-exercise" The thousand-mile range of the TLAM enables a warship well offshore to hold at risk the strategic centers of even land-locked countries.

The USS EISENHOWER (CVN-69) Battle Group Commander receives an operational briefing from his officers. Increasingly, "IT21" — "Information Technology of the 21st Century" — systems are making their way into battle group planning and operations, linking diverse units in a "seamless" web of data and information. The Navy Warfare Development Command in Newport, Rhode Island, for example, is developing a far-reaching concept of operations for network-centric warfare. Linked with the Marine Corp's Warfighting Laboratory in Quantico, in 1999 the Navy's Maritime Battle Center conducted an Extending the Littoral Battlespace technology demonstration for a wireless network connecting ships at sea, aircraft and ground forces. The future is indeed in the Fleet, today.

Right: A "Block IV" Standard Missile leaps from the USS COLE (DDG-67) during a "combined" — multinational — exercise with the German Navy in the Caribbean. The upgraded SM-2 Block IV dramatically increases the engagement capabilities of the Aegis anti-air combat system, and is the "missile of choice" for the Navy's new "Area" Theater Ballistic Missile Defense capability. Coupled with the Lightweight Exo-Atmospheric Projectile — "LEAP"— and a hit-to-kill kinetic-energy warhead, the resulting "Block IV-A" missile will be the heart of the Navy's "Theater-Wide" defense against ballistic missiles...and may serve as an element in a future National Missile Defense system.

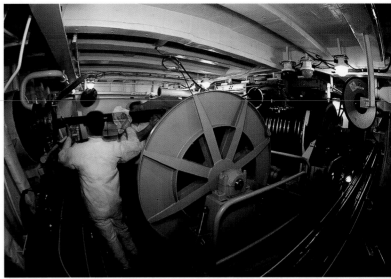

The "threat" lurks somewhere, in the depths. USS Arleigh Burke (DDG-51) launches a lightweight anti-submarine torpedo during an exercise. But before a submarine can be attacked, it must be detected, located, and a fire-control solution fed into the destroyer's weapons.

ABOVE: USS Arleigh Burke is fitted with a Tactical Towed Array Sonar (TACTAS) tail — a 5,600-foot-long array of sensors towed behind the warship to listen to the usually faint tell-tale sounds that every submarine makes, no matter how quiet. The destroyer also can use its bow-mounted sonar in both passive — listen-only — and active — pinging — modes, and can link into various off-board sensors, including sonobuoys dropped from an ASW helicopter or Maritime Patrol Aircraft and advanced deployable sea-bed acoustic arrays, to help in this dangerous cat-and-mouse game.

Action officers in the Combat Information Center — "CIC" — of USS CORONADO (AGF-11) keep a close eye on all developments throughout the littoral battlespace during the Kernel Blitz Maritime Battle Experiment in March 1999. Conducted in conjunction with the Urban Warrior, the experiment tested equipment and concepts of operations for naval support to urban warfare.

A CH-53E Super Stallion helicopter lands on board the USS ESSEX (LHD-2) during an exercise off the California coast. The Sea Stallion is the largest and most powerful helicopter operational outside of Russia, and has been adopted for mine-countermeasures missions as well as heavy-lift and troop-transport tasks.

Top Right: Urban Warrior. A Navy LCAC lands in Oakland, California, testing these assets' capabilities to support maneuver warfare from the sea, when the objective may lie deep within an adversary's coastal population center. The "Three-Block War" concept, in which the Marines will seek to control a small area of an urban center during war, severely stresses current maneuver doctrine, tactics and systems.

Middle Right: U.S. Marines participating in Urban Warrior, in Monterey and San Francisco, California, during Kernel Blitz '99. The exercise tested future command-and-control, fires coordination, and sensor employment for ground and air operations in a constrained urban environment.

Bottom Right: Marines embarking on a CH-53 helicopter from USS BOXER (LHD-4).

A Harrier V/STOL aircraft prepares to launch at
dawn from USS NASSAU (LHA-4) in Norway.

Operations Desert Shield and Desert Storm were the last major conflict in which the largest contingent of Active Duty and Reserve Navy medical department personnel deployed to support Navy and Marine Corps units. Although today's military strategy continues to focus on supporting two simultaneous major theater wars, on a daily basis, Navy medical department personnel are finding themselves deployed worldwide on much smaller scales, for multiple, simultaneous contingencies ranging from humanitarian and disaster relief to operations that take them directly into harm's way. These smaller-scale, more numerous missions — and the casualties that could arise from chemical, biological, radiological, and environmental agents — pose unique challenges to medical teams in delivering care as well as protecting themselves from these very real threats.

Rapid assessment, life-saving interventions, and triage are the hallmarks of combat casualty care. The Hospital Corpsmen in the field providing first-response treatment...the ambulance arriving at the Fleet Hospital with injured Marines and Sailors...the helicopter loaded with casualties landing on board a hospital ship — the Navy medical team plays a significant role in ensuring that Sailors and Marines receive the best medical care anywhere, anytime.

M E D I C I N E

Hospital Corpsmen are the "first responders" in providing medical support to deployed Navy and Marine Corps forces. They also take care of Sailors, Marines, and their families in Navy hospitals and clinics throughout the world. These men and women, whose legacy dates back to 1898 and whose forebears include Medal of Honor recipients, are the cornerstone of Navy Medicine's health-care team.

A typical day for a medical team at sea ranges from conducting sick call or "clinic" to providing emergency, life-saving care for injuries sustained in high-risk shipboard environments. Emergency medical response drills and personnel training are part of the medical department's responsibility at home, at sea, and abroad. Medical department personnel must have comprehensive knowledge of shipboard hazards and the skills needed in damage control and injury prevention. This allows them to institute programs to keep crewmembers alert to hazards and focused on healthy practices, which promote safety and health, and prevent injuries.

The preparation and training of medical department personnel are key to successful support of the varied and challenging military operations facing today's Marines and Sailors.

Commander Jennifer L. Town, NC, USN
Bureau of Medicine and Surgery

Page 100 Top: A volunteer Marine "victim" in a field hospital during exercise Kernel Blitz '99. The ability to quickly get a wounded or injured troop the emergency medical treatment needed often means the difference between saving a life or letting loved-ones know devastating news.

**Page 100 Middle: The Navy's two hospital ships —
USNS Mercy (T-AH-19) and USNS Comfort (T-AH-20) — bring leading-edge medical technologies to forward operating areas. Here, a Navy corpsman practices using a CAT Scan on board Mercy.**

Page 100 Bottom: Navy doctors on board the USNS Mercy treat a patient during a training exercise. Both Mercy and Comfort are maintained in ready-reserve status, one on the east coast (Comfort, in Baltimore, Maryland) and the other on the west coast (Mercy, in Oakland, California). Both ships saw service in the Arabian Gulf during Operations Desert Shield and Desert Storm.

Page 101 Top. Stretcher bearers move patients from a CH-53 helo to Mercy's triage facilities. Converted tankers, both ships are outfitted with 12 operating rooms, four x-ray facilities, a pharmacy, a blood bank, and 80-bed intensive-care facility, and 920 other beds. Another 1,000 additional patients can be given limited care.

Page 101 Bottom. A hospital Corpsman applies moulage for realistic training during exercise Kernel Blitz '99.

UNITY WITHIN

For 40 years UNITAS has stood as a symbol of friendship and cooperation between U.S. Navy and its counterparts in South America. Equally important, it is a highly visible demonstration of the ability of diverse nations to work together to reach a common goal — the defense of mutual interests in this hemisphere.

The first UNITAS cruise in 1959 lasted just 102 days and involved only three weeks of primarily bilateral exercises with the U.S. Navy training with one South American navy after another. A total of 48 ships from Argentina, Brazil, Colombia, Ecuador, Uruguay, Venezuela and the United States participated. Since then, this annual training exercise has grown to nearly five months, involving more than 60 ships, with an operating schedule that involves nearly three months of at-sea training and exercises, much of which is spent in a "combined" — multilateral — operating environment. In 1999, for the first time Argentina, Brazil, and

THE AMERICAS

Uruguay combined their exercises into a single large phase involving 23 ships. Portugal and Spain also sent frigates and more than 36 aircraft to participate in this phase, which brought a European naval dimension to UNITAS.

UNITAS provides an excellent opportunity for international training in amphibious operations, special warfare, anti-submarine warfare, anti-drug smuggling operations, aviation cross-training and more. But the benefits of such exercises go far beyond the opportunity to conduct naval exercises with the United States' South American allies. In-port time sets the stage for lasting friendships. America's Sailors and Marines — "ambassadors of goodwill" in the Southern Hemisphere — routinely go out into local communities to meet with students, compete in international athletic competitions and repair, maintain or construct local schools, churches, and housing projects.

Boatswain mate on O'BANNON readies the ship's deck equipment during UNITAS '99. The USS GUNSTON HALL (LSD-44) steams past the O'BANNON in Puente Arenas, Chile, as a Chilean Navy liaison officer welcomes the destroyer's crew on the ship's fantail.

USS O'Bannon (DD-987), a Spruance (DD-963)-class destroyer, glides through an inland waterway during a 1999 visit to Chile. Port visits and Navy-to-navy exercises are one of the key ways in which the America's Surface Warriors support the U.S. National Security Strategy, National Military Strategy, and the strategies and engagement plans of U.S. regional commanders-in-chief. They enhance the military interoperability and cooperation with America's allies and partners, and also help to

The guided-missile frigate USS STARK (FFG- 31) takes on fuel from a German navy oiler/stores ship during a "combined" — international — training exercise with the Standing NATO Forces Atlantic (SNFL) in the Caribbean during 1999.

Right: The German guided-missile destroyer D-185 launches an SM-1 medium-range Standard Missile during the "missile-ex" phase of training. The D-185 was one of three CHARLES F. ADAMS (DDG-2) class of guided-missile destroyers built in the United States for then-West Germany in the 1960s; another three Adams-class DDGs were built for the Australian navy. The U.S. Navy ultimately acquired 23 of these ships, all of which have been decommissioned and laid up or sold to Greece.

The Canadian frigate MARGARIE in a parade at sea as she readies to leave the group and head home — a tradition for "Sniffle" ships.

Liberty! Join the Navy — See the World! It's not a job — It's an adventure! Let the Voyage Begin! The recruiting slogans ring true as Sailors from America's Heartland "hit" New York City for the first time, after their ship docked for Fourth of July celebrations. Such U.S. port visits are just as important as ship visits to foreign ports: they allow Americans from all walks of life to come on board, to see what their tax dollars have bought, to talk to Sailors about life at sea, and maybe even helps the Navy "close the deal" on a young person uncertain about the future. And it gives America's Sailors opportunities to see parts of the country that perhaps were only images on TV and in magazines. A "win-win" solution!

USS Monsoon (PC-4) steams past a group of seals basking in the sun, as the special-operations patrol craft returns to San Diego harbor en route from a training evolution. Although these ships have been highly successful in their operational assignments, and a fourteenth unit has been added to the fleet, at the U.S. Congress' insistence, seven are being transferred to the U.S. Coast Guard to aid in counter-drug operations in the Caribbean and Gulf of Mexico.

USS Monsoon heads out to sea.

One of MONSOON's petty officers practices using a shoulder-fired Stinger surface-to-air missile, a deadly weapon that proved its worth in the Afghan mujaheddin's struggle against the Soviet Union during the 1980s. Although the specops craft have been criticized as insufficiently armed, with numerous proposals offered to increase their firepower, their real military worth comes from the Naval Special Warfare — "NSW" — SEAL teams that the PCs can insert and extract in covert operations around the globe.

Although most covert and clandestine ops will occur in the dead of a moonless night, practicing during daylight has its advantages. Here, SEALs train with MONSOON's crew in egressing and returning to the craft's fantail.

MONSOON's crew throws a "Killer Tomato — an inflatable target that can take hundreds of hits before sinking" — overboard. The Navy's patrol craft are armed with a variety of small-caliber weapons — 25mm "chain guns," machine guns and grenade launchers — in addition to the Stinger SAMs. Proficiency at these weapons, particularly during high-speed maneuvers, will come only with hundreds of hours of practice.

MONSOON cuts through waves off San Diego. During actual operations, a variety of stealthy measures will help ensure that an adversary's coastal forces will not detect the Navy's patrol craft.

Navy SEALs return to a "RIB" — Rigid-hull Inflatable Boat — manned by Special Boat Unit 26 during a live-fire exercise in Panama. With the turnover of the Panama Canal and U.S. facilities to Panama in early 2000, the Navy and other U.S. Armed Services are increasingly tasked in their ability to "train as they will fight" — which clearly means having realistic terrain and environments, like the jungles of Panama. The issue of access to realistic combined-arms training is one that will only get worse.

American Sailors and Marines have conducted coastal and riverine warfare as far back as America's Revolutionary War. But, it wasn't until the Vietnam War that these dangerous operations were refined to razor-sharpness. Manned by Navy, Marine, and Coast Guard warriors, the U.S. riverine force used heavily armed shallow-draft, high-speed boats to choke off supply lines and strike the enemy in coastal bays, inland rivers, and waterways.

The Navy's most decorated Sailor, Boatswain's Mate Chief James E. Williams, received the Medal of Honor for his selfless courage while serving as Boat Captain and Patrol Officer of PBR-105 on the Mekong River in Vietnam on 31 October 1966. After more than three hours of fierce battle, Williams' patrol had accounted for the destruction or loss of 65 enemy boats and more than 1,000 enemy troops.

A "Sea Specter" PB MK III patrol boat cuts through a Panamanian waterway. The "Mark-Threes" have now been replaced by the much more capable, stealthy, high-speed, high-firepower, shallow-draft MK V Special Operations Craft. The 45-knot-plus MK Vs have an unrefueled range of some 500 nautical miles, are operated by five-man crews, and are capable of carrying a 16-man SEAL platoon with four Combat Rubber Raiding Craft.

In addition to earning the Medal of Honor, Chief Williams awards include three Purple Hearts, three Bronze Stars, the Vietnamese Cross of Gallantry, the Navy and Marine Corps Medal, two Silver Stars, and the Navy Cross. He died on 13 October 1999 — the Navy's 224th Birthday.

Although today the "brown water" Navy tends to be associated with operations in Vietnam, this type of warfare must not be discounted in the 21st century. With the dramatically increasing range of the Navy's and possible adversaries' weapons, "littoral" has come to mean many hundreds of miles at sea — not solely "brown water."

In the future, even more advanced, stealthy and high-firepower craft will be integral elements of U.S. naval strategies and operations — particularly in support of over-the-horizon amphibious assaults.

At the dawn of the new century, the Navy can and does expect to encounter a wide spectrum of mines, from low-tech contact mines to the most technologically sophisticated, multiple-influence weapons, some of which are rocket-propelled to allow attacks from great distances. Modern influence mines, which can be actuated by magnetic, acoustic, seismic, underwater electrical potential, pressure, or virtually any combination of permutation of all such ship "signatures," increasingly incorporate advanced technologies and microprocessors that significantly improves their lethality, versatility, and reliability. Some are even designed with "stealth" technologies — including irregular shapes, sound-deadening anechoic coatings, and non-magnetic materials — to decrease the likelihood that they can be defeated by mine countermeasures operations.

"Where the Fleet Goes, the Mine Warfare Force Has Already Been" —
the motto of the U.S. Navy's mine countermeasures (MCM) force. The
MCM ship USS Avenger (MCM-1) and USS Inchon (MCS-12), the Navy's
sole MCM command, control, and support ship, work up in the Gulf
of Mexico, off Ingleside, Texas. The Headquarters of the Commander,
Mine Warfare Command, is located at Ingleside, across the bay from
Naval Air Station Corpus Christi, and serves as the Navy's mine warfare center of excellence. On the other side of the Gulf of Mexico, at
Panama City, Florida, the engineers and technicians at the Navy's
Coastal Systems Station help to perfect the technologies, systems,
tactics, techniques and procedures to neutralize the deadly threat of
naval mines — weapons that wait.

A Navy EOD diver attaches explosive training devices to a dummy contact mine similar to the type that nearly sank USS SAMUEL B.ROBERTS (FFG-58) and severely damaged USS TRIPOLI (LPH-10) in the Arabian Gulf in 1991. Once a moored mine is cut free and floats to the surface, EOD divers can render it safe — allowing the mine to be "exploited" by engineers in the Navy's labs — or "neutralize" it by attaching explosive charges and destroying it.

Top Left: USS SCOUT (MCM-8) prepares to deploy a "Slick-48" — SLQ-48 Mine Neutralization System (MNS) — mine-hunting robot into the water. After a "mine-like object" has been detected and then classified as a mine by the ship's sonar, the MNS is "flown" by an operator on board the ship to the position of target. Attached to the ship by a 3,500-foot umbilical cable, the MNS carries a small sonar and a low-light-level television camera for examining the target and determining the type of mine. It can destroy bottom mines by placing an explosive charge near the mine or cutting the cable of moored mines, causing them to rise to the surface, where they can be neutralized or rendered-safe for "exploitation" — gathering critical intelligence about the threat. This "exploitation" function is often overlooked by all except the MCM "professionals," but is critically important. One of the mines the Navy encountered during Operation Desert Storm was a very sophisticated multiple-influence Soviet/Russian weapon not seen before in the West.

Bottom Left: Often the only way a target can be classified is to put a diver — or specially trained bottlenose dolphins — into the water. Here, EOD divers using a PCS-2 hand-held sonar approach a practice mine. EOD divers rely on the Mk-16 Underwater Breathing Apparatus — UBA — and acoustically silent ("no bubbles, no troubles") and magnetically neutral rebreathing system to allow them to work in close proximity to bottom or moored mines — safely!

A Surface Warrior on board INCHON, on lookout in the fog. Despite all the high-technology systems that are, or soon will be, available to the operating forces, often the first detection of a mine is by the "Mark-One Eyeball," so lookouts are routinely posted if a mine threat is suspected. Such was the situation facing the USS SAMUEL B. ROBERTS in April 1988 — "Captain!" a lookout shouted, "we're in the middle of a minefield!" Too late...the mine exploded causing extensive damage to the ship.

Top Left: Female fireman pauses during Flight Ops on board USS INCHON. A former amphibious assault ship (LPH), Inchon was converted and modernized in the mid-1990s as a result of the mine countermeasures lessons-learned during Operation Desert Storm in 1991 and the subsequent mine-clearance operations that extended well into 1992. The ship now has state-of-the-art "C4ISR" — command, control, communications, computers, intelligence, surveillance, and reconnaissance — capabilities to support an MCM squadron commander and staff. Inchon also provides the operating base for an embarked Airborne MCM helicopter squadron of eight MH-53E Sea Dragon AMCM helicopters and EOD MCM detachments, as well as the logistics and maintenance support for surface MCM ships.

Bottom Left: An MH-53E Sea Dragon helo lifts off from USS INCHON. The Sea Dragon can tow advanced mine-hunting sonars, to determine the presence of mines, and can operate a variety of mechanical and influence minesweeping equipment to neutralize them. In addition to operating from Inchon, the MH-53Es and their supporting equipment and personnel are capable of being airlifted by C-5B strategic airlift aircraft practically anywhere in the world, and can be set up and operating from advanced, austere facilities within a matter of days.

Sea Dragons at rest on board USS INCHON at dusk. Still, if the mission and threat demand it, the Navy's MH-53Es can operate around the clock. Because of the excellent MCM capabilities of these "dedicated" AMCM helicopters, the Navy is looking at modifications to the Seahawk CH-60 multi-mission helicopter to provide "organic" AMCM capabilities to virtually any warship or even auxiliaries that can operate these smaller and lighter helos.

A crewman trains a high-pressure fire hose on the nearby training hulk. The Navy's salvage and rescue ships are expected to perform a numerous missions, in addition to locating and recovering wreckage — of ships, boats, and aircraft — or sometimes errant weapons or other equipment on the ocean floor. Only a decade ago the Navy's salvage and rescue fleet numbered some 20 ships; today the Service's "organic" capabilities reside in just four ships — two homeported on the east coast and two on the west coast — and in the past five years the demand on these assets has been non-stop.

Previous Page: USS GRASP (ARS-51) engaged in a fire-fighting exercise in the Chesapeake Bay.

Instructors and emergency medical personnel observe Navy divers inside a recompression chamber at the Navy's dive school, located at Panama City, Florida. Novice divers are monitored closely to see whether they are likely to be challenged by the physical and psychological stress they will encounter in the real world.

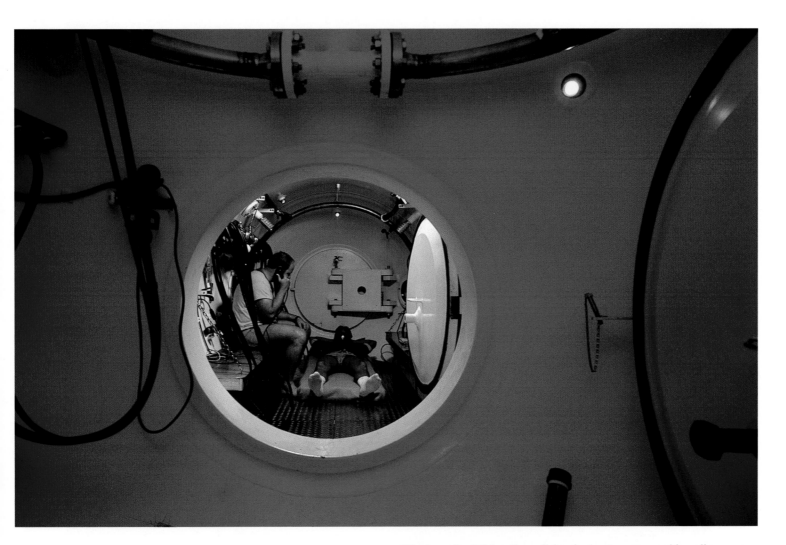

"Yeah, we're OK," a Navy diving instructor assures his colleagues outside the recompression chamber.

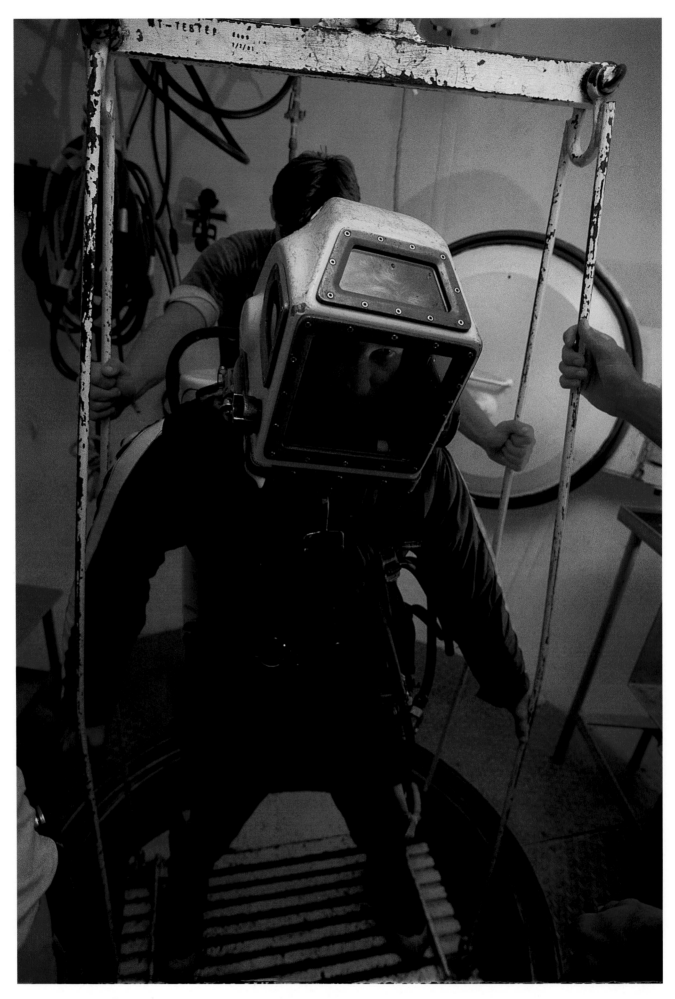

The Experimental Diving Unit — EDU — is a critically important element of the Navy's diving programs at Panama City. The EDU is a specialized detachment of highly skilled divers, engineers, and scientists who address physiological and psychological aspects, as well as new equipment and techniques, of diving in all climates and environments. Here, Navy divers ready for a test inside the EDU's recompression chamber.

It's almost as stressful as a Navy "nugget" aviator's first solo flight, the first open-water dive for a Navy trainee. The good climate in the Gulf of Mexico, with only the occasional hurricane to disrupt schedules, allows training to continue throughout the year.

"Are you OK?" a U.S. Navy salvage dive instructor asks a Thai navy diver — using the universal hand-symbol for "OK" — during Exercise CARAT 99. A flyaway dive locker and portable recompression chamber can be seen in the background, just in case someone gets in trouble. One of the important roles for the Navy's diving and salvage community includes training and exercising with the divers of America's allies and friends worldwide. Because of the significant "down-sizing" of the U.S. diving and salvage force, it makes good sense to have other nations' diving and salvage forces capable of assisting the Navy in an emergency.

Left: Vital research is conducted and data collected at the Naval Medical Research Institute (NMRI) at the National Naval Medical Center (NNMC) in Bethesda, Maryland. In this test of an experimental electrical thermal suit, a Navy diver has been placed in extremely cold water for several hours, and has been directed to carry out increasingly difficult tasks that would be encountered in a real-world operation. Commissioned on 27 October 1942, today NMRI supports the National Naval Medical Center, Naval Health Sciences Education and Training Command, and the Uniformed Services University of Health Sciences, and it links with the Bureau of Medicine and Surgery (BUMED). NMRI's work focuses primarily on the development and testing of devices and methods to be used by the Fleet. Extensive studies have been performed on protective clothing, desalination, aviation, oxygen equipment, insect repellents, cold-water immersion, vaccines, night vision, body armor, nutrition, oral hygiene, tropical diseases and parasites. NMRI combines the work of scientists, doctors, and engineers from academic, commercial and naval laboratories. NMRI's Diving and Environmental Physiology Department conducts research on human performance during military operations, including decompression sickness and oxygen toxicity. The decompression program does saturation research, decompression procedures, model development of gas exchange and bubble dynamics and the control of contaminants in confined atmospheres.

An engineer inspects one of the massive five-bladed propellers of the 33rd ARLEIGH BURKE (DDG-51)-class Aegis guided-missile destroyer, USS HOWARD (DDG-83), at Bath Iron Works (BIW), Bath, Maine. Each of the ship's props are linked to two gas-turbine propulsion systems, together generating a combined 100,000 shaft horsepower that can drive the destroyer at speeds in excess of 32 knots. The variable-pitch, reversing props will allow the commanding officer order a "crash-back" evolution that will have the ship go from all-ahead full to all-astern in a matter of minutes, sometimes resulting in a wave of "green water" crashing over the transom — thoroughly drenching anyone unlucky enough to be on the fantail at the time. Bath Iron Works is the last major U.S. shipyard that builds its warship on "ways" and rails on which the nearly completed ship will be slid into the water, stern-first, when it is launched.

An example of somewhat more modern warship construction at Bath Iron Works, Bath, Maine. Aegis destroyers are fabricated in modules and the modules are fitted and welded together, after which the ship is floated — not launched! — at its christening. Still, it takes millions of man- and woman-hours to build a modern warship, one of the most complex items ever constructed.

HOWARD gathers speed as she slides toward the Kennebec River on 20 November 1999. The DDG-83 is named in honor of Marine Corps Gunnery Sergeant Jimmie E. Howard (1929-1993), recipient of the Medal of Honor for his courage and leadership during the Vietnam War.

"Man the blocks!" A time-honored tradition at BIW, construction workers, pipefitters, outfitters, uniformed and civilian Navy people, contractors, even naval analysts and writers join teams to drive heavy steel rods into chocks that — little by little — will raise the 8,300-ton warship ever-so-slightly off the rails.

The ship is then held in place, almost perilously, poised for the moment that her sponsor will announce, "I christen you USS HOWARD!", and crash a bottle of Champagne on the warship's bow...sending her on the first leg of a voyage that will almost certainly see the ship respond to crisis and conflict numerous times during her 35-year life.

Admiral Arleigh "31-Knot" Burke

"This ship is built to fight...you better know how!" So declared Admiral Arleigh "31-Knot" Burke, World War II Navy Destroyerman and former Chief of Naval Operations, during a special keel-laying ceremony in July 1986. To then-Commander John Morgan, USN, prospective commanding officer of the USS Arleigh Burke (DDG-51), lead ship of the multimission Aegis guided missile destroyer class, and his still-forming crew, they were words that burned into their hearts...their souls. The Admiral's words would guide them as they trained for the day they would first take their ship to sea. And they inspired the skilled tradesmen and women at Bath Iron Works and Ingalls Shipbuilding who labored to fashion thousands of tons of steel and cable and armor and paint and fabric into living warships worthy of the name Burke.

U.S. Navy

The state-of-the-art DDG-51 destroyers have combat systems centered on the Aegis Weapon System and the SPY-1D multi-function, phased-array radar. Arleigh Burke's combat system includes the Mk 41 Vertical Launching System, an advanced anti-submarine warfare system, highly capable anti-air warfare missiles, and long-range Tomahawk land-attack cruise missiles. These ships will soon be fitted with area-wide defense against ballistic and overland cruise missiles. Incorporating all-steel construction and gas-turbine propulsion, DDG-51 destroyers provide multi-mission offensive and defensive capabilities, and operate independently or as part of carrier battle groups, surface action groups, amphibious ready groups, and underway replenishment groups. The "Flight IIA" upgrade incorporates facilities to support two embarked helicopters, significantly enhancing the ship's sea-control capabilities. A total of 57 DDG-51s are in the Navy's plan, and through 1999, 28 DDG-51s had been delivered to the Navy. The real-world experiences of these ships in crisis and conflict from the Adriatic to the Taiwan Straits have demonstrated that these ships were built to fight. And the men and women of their crews indeed know how.

The grandson of a Swedish immigrant, Burke was born on a farm near Boulder, Colorado on 19 October 1901. He entered the Naval Academy in June 1919 and graduated on 7 June 1923, standing 71 in a

USS Arleigh Burke (DDG-51) at flank speed

class of 413. Following graduation Burke served in a variety of afloat and ashore jobs, finding that he excelled in naval gunnery, and supported the development of high-speed night gunnery and torpedo attack tactics — skills that would be critical during the war.

In October 1943, Captain Burke took over DESTROYER SQUADRON 23 ("Little Beavers") in October. During the next four months the squadron participated in 22 separate engagements and destroyed one Japanese cruiser, nine destroyers, one submarine, several smaller ships and approximately 30 aircraft. The ships of the time were capable of 34 knots, but while enroute to a rendezvous prior to the Battle of Cape St. George, a boiler casualty had limited his group's top speed to 30 knots. When the fleet commander signalled him to make best speed, they mustered an extra knot, and he answered "Proceeding at 31 knots." The subsequent fleet commander's response, addressed to "31-knot" Burke, was a "rib," but captured the imagination of the press and the public and conveyed the image of a dashing, hard-charging combat commander.

After a brief tour in the Bureau of Ordnance following the end of the war, Burke returned to sea, all too briefly, and received an unexpected set of orders to report immediately to the staff of the Chief of Naval Operations (OPNAV) in Washington to head the OPNAV section that dealt with matters concerning unification of the armed services.

Following the inauguration of President Eisenhower in January 1953 and the introduction of the "New Look" defense policy, Burke was called upon to help define and defend the Navy's roles, missions, and command structure and philosophy. In May 1955 President Eisenhower selected Burke over 99 officers senior to him — every four- and three-star officer in the Navy and several senior two-star officers — to relieve Admiral Robert Carney as the Chief of Naval Operations.

Upon becoming CNO on 17 August 1955, one of Burke's highest priorities was the development of a solid propellant fleet ballistic missile. He established the Special Projects Office, appointed Rear Admiral William Raborn as head, and gave him wide latitude to accomplish the objective. Polaris was the result. Another priority was construction of nuclear powered surface ships — carriers, cruisers, and destroyers. The nuclear-power guided missile cruiser USS Long Beach (CGN-9) and aircraft carrier USS Enterprise (CVN-65) were authorized and built, and other nuclear warships followed. He pressed for conversion of cruisers to employ guided missiles and these new weapons' introduction in other ships to defend against air attack. As a response to the burgeoning Soviet submarine fleet, he accelerated anti-submarine warfare programs were accelerated. On 25 July 1961, in ceremonies at the U.S. Naval Academy where he had graduated 38 years earlier, Admiral Burke was relieved as the Chief of Naval Operations and retired. He was, and remains, the longest-serving Chief of Naval Operations in the history of the U.S. Navy.

"Sailor." Admiral Burke, famed World War II destroyerman and former Chief of Naval Operations, with his wife, Roberta — "Bobbie" — at the commissioning of USS Arleigh Burke (DDG-51) on the Fourth of July 1991. Renown for his heroism and exploits in the Pacific Theater of Operations, Admiral Burke was equally respected for guiding the Navy into the missile and nuclear "age."

USS Stephan W. Groves (FFG-29) sails
through the inland water in Chile

As heart wrenching as the day of departure was six months earlier, for the Sailors aboard USS Phillipine Sea "CG-58" today is a time for joyful reunions and catching up. Although today's Sailors have "e-mail" and even "local" telephone calls from forward operating areas — assuming the ship and the satellite are in the right position! — nothing can compare to "He's got my nose!" A Sailor serving America on board USS Truett (FF-1095) meets his newborn baby for the first time.

An MV-22 Osprey tilt-rotor aircraft conducts sea trials from the USS SAIPAN (LHA-2). The Osprey is a Vertical/Short Take-Off or Landing (V/STOL) aircraft designed as the medium-lift replacement for the Services' aging CH-46E and CH-53D helicopters. Incorporating advanced technologies in composite materials, survivability, airfoil design, fly-by-wire controls, digital avionics, and manufacturing, the MV-22 is capable of carrying 24 combat-equipped Marines or a 10,000-pound external load, and has a strategic self-deployment capability of 2,100 nautical miles with a single aerial refueling. The MV-22's 38-foot rotor system and engine/transmission nacelle mounted on each wingtip allow it to operate as a helicopter for take-off and landing. Once airborne, the nacelles rotate forward 90 degrees, converting the MV-22 intoa high-speed, high-altitude, fuel-efficient turboprop aircraft.

The MV-22 represents a revolutionary change in aircraft capability to meet expeditionary mobility needs for the 21st century. A Special Operation Forces variant, CV-22, is also under development for the Air Force. The total buy for the Marine Corps, Navy and Air Force is 458 aircraft, 360 of which are earmarked for the Marines. The U.S. Coast Guard is looking into a smaller variant of the V-22 as a replacement for its helicopter and medium-range aircraft assets intended for deepwater operations.

Twenty-first century naval warfare demands the ability to "reach out and touch" America's adversaries — whether terrorist groups operating with hoped-for impunity from mountaintop havens or land-locked "rogue states" — from the sea. The Navy's new-design Land-Attack Destroyer (DD-21) is the first surface warship founded entirely upon post-Cold War thinking and strategic concepts of "joint" — multi-Service — operations in the "littoral conflict environment" and addresses the need to directly support forces ashore and hold at risk targets far inland...anywhere, any time. Armed with a lethal array of land-attack weapons — including the Advanced Land-Attack Missile, Tactical Tomahawk cruise missile, and the Advanced Gun System firing Extended-Range Guided Munitions — DD-21 will provide sustained, accurate, and precise firepower at long ranges.

Land-Attack Destroyer (DD-21)

Innovation and change have been embraced throughout the ship, from its integrated electric-drive propulsion, to automated damage-control sensors and systems, to a ship-wide fiber-optic local-area-network that links all communications, command, and control systems into an interconnected web that will ensure information superiority to meet the daunting needs of the future.

Advanced offensive and defensive combat systems — perhaps including high-powered lasers and electromagnetic guns in future ships — are much more likely now that the Navy has decided on electric drive for DD-21, the first ship of what ultimately may be called the "All-Electric Navy."

DD-21 concept illustration courtesy of © United Defense

T E C H N I C A L

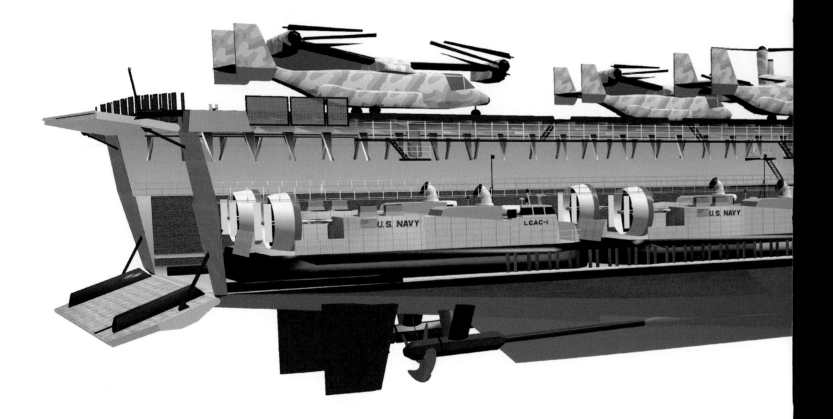

San Antonio Class Amphibious Assault Ship (LPD-17)

"The LPD-17 is the tip of the spear for tomorrow's expeditionary warfare operations," enthused Major General Dennis Krupp, the Director of Expeditionary Warfare (N85) in the Office of the Chief of Naval Operations. "It embodies the renaissance in amphibious doctrine and operations that are the core of the Navy-Marine Corps Team in the 21st century."

The new San Antonio LPD is an amphibious transport dock ship designed, engineered, and crafted for operational flexibility to meet Marine Air-Ground Task Force (MAGTF) lift requirements in the emerging Operational Maneuver from the Sea (OMFTS) and Ship-to-Objective Maneuver (STOM) concepts of operations. It is a medium-size — approximately 25,000 tons full load — medium-speed — greater than 20 knots, sustained — diesel-powered ship, 684 feet in length, with a beam of 105 feet and an estimated crew of 363. When the lead LPD-17 reaches the Fleet in 2004, it will carry approximately

A P P E N D I C E S

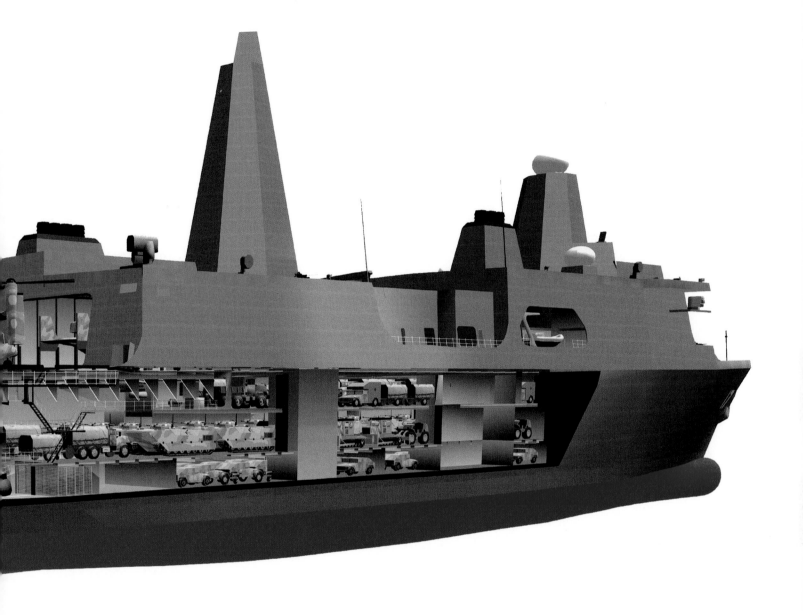

720 troops and will have 25,000 square feet of space for vehicles, 36,000 cubic feet of cargo space, medical facilities (24 beds, two operating rooms), aviation facilities for a mix of helicopter and tilt-rotor aircraft), and two landing craft air cushion (LCAC) vehicles.

The 12 LPD-17s in the program will provide the functional replacement for 36 aging amphibious lift ships. In conjunction with the Wasp (LHD-1)-class, and Tarawa (LHA-1)-class amphibious assault ships, and 12 Whidbey Island and Harpers Ferry landing ship docks (LSDs), the Navy will have the foundation for meeting the assault-echelon lift requirements of 2.5 Marine Expeditionary Brigade (MEB) equivalents during wartime and sustaining approximately three forward-deployed Marine Expeditionary Units (MEUs) in peacetime. The LPDs are being built by the Avondale Alliance, which comprises Avondale Industries, New Orleans, Louisiana; Bath Iron Works, Bath, Maine; Raytheon, San Diego, California; and Intergraph, Huntsville, Alabama.

TECHNICAL

APPENDICES

The information compiled in these appendices was obtained from The US Navy Office of Information.

More information can be obtained from the Navy web site at:
http://www.navy.mil.
Surface Navy Association at:
http://www.navysna.org
U.S. Naval Institute at:
http://www.usni.org
Naval Historical Center at:
http://www.history.navy.mil/index
Naval Historical Foundation at:
http://www.mil.org/navyhist/index.htm
world wide web virtual library, naval and maritime at:
http://www.iit.edu/~vlnavmar/

AEGIS COMBAT SYSTEM

The Aegis system was designed as a total weapon system, from detection to kill. The heart of the system is an advanced, automatic detect and track, multi-function phased-array radar, the AN/SPY-1. This high powered (four megawatt) radar is able to perform search, track and missile guidance functions simultaneously with a track capacity of over 100 targets. The first Engineering Development Model (EDM-1) was installed in the test ship, *USS Norton Sound* (AVM 1) in 1973.

The computer-based command and decision element is the core of the Aegis combat system. This interface makes the Aegis combat system capable of simultaneous operation against a multi-mission threat: anti-air, anti-surface and anti-submarine warfare.

The Navy built the first Aegis cruisers using the hull and machinery designs of *Spruance* class destroyers. The commissioning of *USS Bunker Hill* (CG 52) opened a new era in surface warfare as the first Aegis ship outfitted with the Vertical Launching System (VLS), allowing greater missile selection,firepower and surviv-

ability. The improved AN/SPY-1B radar went to sea in *USS Princeton* (CG 59), ushering in another advance in Aegis capabilities. *USS Chosin* (CG 65) introduced the AN/UYK-43/44 computers, which provide increased processing capabilities.

In 1980, a smaller ship was designed using an improved sea-keeping hull form, reduced infra-red and radar cross section and upgrades to the Aegis Combat System. The first ship of the DDG 51 class, *Arleigh Burke*, was commissioned on the Fourth of July, 1991. The DDG 51 class was named after a living person, the legendary Adm. Arleigh Burke, the most famous destroyerman of World War II.

DDG 51s were constructed in flights, allowing technological advances during construction. Flight II, introduced in FY 1992, incorporates improvements to the SPY radar and the Standard missile, active electronic counter-measures and communications. Flight IIA, introduced in fiscal year 1994, added a helicopter hangar with one anti-submarine helicopter and one-armed attack helicopter. The Aegis program has also projected reducing the cost of each Flight IIA ship by at least $30 million.

AMMUNITION SHIPS - AE

Ammunition ships deliver munitions to warships.

Features: Ammunition ships keep the fleet supplied with ammunition and ordnance, independently or with other combat logistic ships. Ammunition is delivered by slings on ship-to-ship cables, and by helicopters.

Background: The Navy's ammunition ships are all of the *Kilauea* class. The lead ship of the class, *USNS Kilauea* (T-AE 26), along with *USNS Butte* (T-AE 27), *USNS Santa Barbara* (T-AE 28), *USNS Flint* (T-AE 32), *USNS Shasta* (T-AE 33)*USNS Mount Baker* (T-AE 34) and *USNS Kiska* (T-AE 35) are operated by the Military Sealift Command with a civilian master and crew, but the remaining one is Navy manned with a commanding officer.

GENERAL CHARACTERISTICS, *KILUAUEA* CLASS

Builder: AE-29, Bethlehem Steel, Sparrows Point, MD.
Power Plant: Three boilers, geared turbines, one shaft, 22,000 shaft horsepower
Length: 564 feet (171.91meters)
Beam: 81 feet (24.69 meters)
Displacement: Approximately 18,088 long tons (18,378.28 metric tons) full load
Speed: 20 knots (23+ miles, 37.01+ km, per hour)
Aircraft: Two CH-*46 Sea Knight* helicopters

SHIPS:

Homeport: Bremerton, Washington
USS Mount Hood (AE-9)

Crew: 17 officers, 366 enlisted
Armament: Two *Phalanx* close-in-weapons systems
Date deployed: 14 December 1968 *(USS Butte)*

AMPHIBIOUS ASSAULT SHIPS, LHA/LHD

Primary landing ships, resembling small aircraft carriers, designed to put troops on hostile shores.

Features: Modern U.S. Navy amphibious assault ships are called upon to perform as primary landing ships for assault operations of Marine expeditionary units. These ships use Landing Craft Air Cushion *(LCAC)*, conventional landing craft and helicopters to move Marine assault forces ashore. In a secondary role, using AV-8B *Harrier* aircraft and anti-submarine warfare helicopters, these ships perform sea control and limited power projection missions.

Background: Amphibious warships are uniquely designed to support assault from the sea against defended positions ashore. They must be able to sail in harm's way and provide a rapid built-up of combat power ashore in the face of opposition. The United States maintains the largest and most capable amphibious force in the world. The *Wasp*-class are the largest amphibious ships in the world. The lead ship, *USS Wasp* (LHD-1), was commissioned in July 1989 in Norfolk, Va.

The Guam (LPH 9), the last of the *Iwo Jima* Class, was decommissioned August 25,1998.

GENERAL CHARACTERISTICS, *WASP* CLASS

Builder: Ingalls Shipbuilding, Pascagoula, Mississippi
Power Plant: Two boilers, two geared steam turbines, two shafts, 70,000 shaft horsepower
Length: 844 feet (257.30 meters)
Beam: 106 feet (32.31 meters)
Displacement: Approx. 40,500 long tons (41,150 metric tons) full load
Speed: 20+ knots (23+ miles per hour)
Aircraft:
Assault: 42 CH-46 *Sea Knight* helicopters
Sea Control: 5 AV-8B *Harrier* attack planes; Six ASW helicopters

SHIPS:

Homeport: Norfolk, VA.
USS Wasp (LHD-1)
USS Bataan (LHD-5)
USS Kearsarge (LHD-3)
Homeport: San Diego, CA.
USS Essex (LHD-2),
USS Boxer (LHD-4),
USS Bonhomme Richard (LHD-6),

Crew: Ships Company: 104 officers, 1,004 enlisted
Marine Detachment: 1,894
Armament: Two NATO Sea Sparrow launchers; three 20mm *Phalanx* CIWS mounts; eight .50 cal. machine guns
Date Deployed: July 29, 1989 *(USS Wasp)*

GENERAL CHARACTERISTICS, *TARAWA* CLASS

Builders: Ingalls Shipbuilding, Pascagoula, Mississippi.
Power Plant: Two boilers, two geared steam turbines, two shafts, 70,000 total shaft horsepower
Length: 820 feet (249.94 meters)
Beam: 106 feet (32.31 meters)
Displacement: 39,400 long tons (40,032 metric tons) full load
Speed: 24 knots (27.62 miles per hour)
Aircraft: *(Actual mix depends upon mission)*
Nine CH-53 *Sea Stallion* helicopters, Twelve CH-46 *Sea Knight* helicopters, Six AV-8B *Harrier* attack planes

SHIPS:

Homeport: San Diego, CA.
USS Tarawa (LHA-1)
USS Peleliu (LHA-5)
Homeport: Norfolk, VA.
USS Saipan (LHA-2),
USS Nassau (LHA-4)
Homeport: Sasebo, Japan
USS Belleau Wood (LHA-3),

Crew:
Ships Company: 82 officers, 882 enlisted Marine Detachment 1,900 plus
Armament: Two RAM launchers; two 5 inch/54 cal. MK-45 lightweight guns; two *Phalanx* 20 mm CIWS mount; six 25 mm MK-38 machine guns
Date Deployed: May 29, 1976 *(USS Tarawa)*

AMPHIBIOUS COMMAND SHIPS – LCC

Amphibious Command ships provide command and control for fleet commanders.

Background: Commissioned in 1970, these are the only ships to be designed initially for an amphibious command ship role. Earlier amphibious command ships lacked sufficient speed to keep up with a 20-knot amphibious force. Subsequently, both ships became fleet flagships. *USS Blue Ridge* became the Seventh Fleet command ship in 1979, and *USS Mount Whitney* became the Second Fleet command ship in 1981.

GENERAL CHARACTERISTICS, *BLUE RIDGE* CLASS

Builders: Philadelphia Naval Shipyard - LCC 19
Newport News Shipbuilding and Drydock Co. - LCC 20.
Power Plant: Two boilers, one geared turbine, one shaft; 22,000 horsepower
Length overall: 634 feet (193.24 meters)
Beam extreme: 108 feet (32.92 meters)
Displacement: 18,874 long tons (19,176.89 metric tons) full load
Speed: 23 knots (26.5+ miles, 42.65+ km, per hour)
Aircraft: All helicopters except the CH-53 *Sea Stallion* can be carried

SHIPS:

Homeport: Yokuska, Japan
USS Blue Ridge (LCC-19)
Homeport: Norfolk, VA.
USS Mount Whitney (LCC-20)

Crew: 52 officers, 790 enlisted
Date Deployed: 14 November 1970 *(USS Blue Ridge)*

AMPHIBIOUS TRANSPORT DOCK - LPD

Troop transports for amphibious operations

Features: The amphibious transports are use to transport and land Marines, their equipment and supplies by embarked landing craft or amphibious vehicles augmented by helicopters in amphibious assault.

Background: These versatile ships perform the mission of amphibious transports, amphibious cargo ships and the older LSDs.

GENERAL CHARACTERISTICS *AUSTIN* CLASS

Builders:
LPD 4-6, New York Naval Shipyard
LPD 7 and LPD 8, Ingalls Shipbuilding
LPD 9, 10, 12-15, Lockheed Shipbuilding
Unit cost: $235-419 million
Power plant: Two boilers, two steam turbines, two shafts, 24,000 shaft horsepower
Length: 570 feet (173.74 meters)
Beam: 84 feet (25.60 meters)
Displacement: Approximately 17,000 long tons (17,272.82 metric tons) full load
Speed: 21 knots (24.20+ mph, 38.95 kph)
Aircraft: Up to six CH-46 Sea Knight helicopters

SHIPS:

Homeport, San Diego
USS Ogden (LPD 5)
USS Duluth (LPD 6)
USS Cleveland (LPD 7)
USS Dubuque (LPD 8)
USS Denver (LPD 9)
Homeport, Norfolk, VA.
USS Shreveport (LPD 12)
USS Nashville (LPD 13)
USS Trenton (LPD 14)
USS Ponce (LPD 15)
USS Austin (LPD 4)

Homeport: Sasebo, Japan
USS Juneau (LPD 10)

Crew:
Ship's Company: 420 (24 officers, 396 enlisted)
Marine Detachment: 900
Armament: Two 25mm Mk 38 guns; two Phalanx CIWS; and eight .50-calibre machine guns.
Date Deployed: Feb. 6, 1965 *(USS Austin)*

COASTAL MINE HUNTERS – MHC

Ships designed to clear mines from vital waterways.

Background: In the early 1980s, the U.S. Navy began development of a new mine countermeasures (MCM) force, which included two new classes of ships and minesweeping helicopters. The vital importance of a state-of-the-art mine countermeasures force was strongly underscored in the Persian Gulf during the eight years of the Iran-Iraq war, and in *Operations Desert Shield* and *Desert Storm* in 1990 and 1991. To learn more about Mine Warfare visit their command's web site.

Osprey (MHC 51) class ships are mine hunter-killers capable of finding, classifying and destroying moored and bottom mines. The MHC 51 has a 15-day endurance and depends on a support ship or shore based facilities for resupply.

Avenger class ships are also designed as mine hunter-killers.
These ships use sonar and video systems, cable cutters and a mine detonating device that can be released and detonated by remote control. They are also capable of conventional sweeping measures. The ships' hulls are made of glass-reinforced plastic (GRP) fiberglass. They are the first large mine countermeasures ships built in the United States in nearly 27 years.

GENERAL CHARACTERISTICS, *OSPREY* CLASS

Builders:
MHC 51, 52, 55, 58, 59, 60 and 61 Intermarine USA, Savannah, GA

MHC 53, 54, 56, 57 Avondale Industries Inc., Gulfport, MS
Power Plant: Two diesels (800 hp each); two Voith-Schneider (cycloidal) propulsion systems
Length: 188 feet (57.30 meters)
Beam: 36 feet (10.97 meters)
Displacement: 893 long tons (907.33 metric tons) full load
Speed: 10 knots (11.51 mph, 18.52 kmph)

SHIPS:

Homeport, Ingleside, TX.
USS Osprey (MHC 51)
USS Heron (MHC 52)
USS Pelican (MHC 53)
USS Robin (MHC 54)
USS Oriole (MHC 55)
USS Kingfisher (MHC 56)
USS Cormorant (MHC 57)
USS Black Hawk (MHC 58)
USS Falcon (MHC 59)
USS Cardinal (MHC 60)
USS Raven (MHC 61)
USS Shrike (MHC 62)

Crew: 5 officers, 46 enlisted
Armament: Two .50 caliber machine guns, Mine Neutralization System and other mine countermeasures systems
Date Deployed: 20 Nov 1993 *(USS Osprey)*

COMMAND SHIP - AGF

Command ships serve as the flagships for the Commander, Third Fleet, and Commander, Sixth Fleet.

Features: Command ships provide communications and accommodations for fleet commanders and staff. Ships are equipped air and surface radars, helicopter, chaff launchers, and an electronic warfare suite.
Background: These ships were converted from amphibious warfare ships for employment as command ships.

GENERAL CHARACTERISTICS, *LA SALLE* CLASS

Builders: (as LPD-3) New York Naval Shipyard, N.Y.
Conversion: (to AGF-3) Philadelphia Navy Yard, Philadelphia, Penn.
Power Plant: Two boilers, geared turbines, two shafts, 24,000 shaft horsepower
Length: 520 feet (158.5 meters)

Beam: 84 feet (26.60 meters)
Displacement: 14,650 tons (14,885.10 metric tons)
Speed: 20 knots (23.82+ miles per hour)
Aircraft: one light helicopter
Ship: USS La Salle (AGF 3), Forward deployed to Gaeta, Italy.
Crew: 440 ships company + 59 flag staff
Armament: 2 *Phalanx* close-in-weapons system, four machine gun mounts, two saluting guns

GENERAL CHARACTERISTICS, *CORONADO* CLASS

Builders: (as LPD-11) Lockheed Shipbuilding & Construction Co.
Conversion: (to AGF-11) Philadelphia Navy Yard, Philadelphia, Penn.
Power Plant: two boilers, geared turbines, twin shafts, 24,000 shaft horsepower
Length: 570 feet (173.74 meters)
Beam: 100 feet (30.48 meters)
Displacement: 16,912 long tons (17,183.41 metric tons)
Speed: 21 knots (24.2+ miles per hour, 38.95+ kph)
Aircraft: two light helicopters

SHIP:

Homeport: San Diego, CA.
USS Coronado (AGF 11)
Homeport: Gaeta, Italy
USS LaSalle (AGF 3)

Crew: 516 ships company + 120 flag staff
Armament: two *Phalanx* close-in-weapons system, two 12.7 mm MGs

---

CRUISERS - CG

Large combat vessel with multiple target response capability.

Features: Modern U. S. Navy guided missile cruisers perform primarily in a Battle Force role. These ships are multi-mission (AAW, ASW, ASUW) surface combatants capable of supporting carrier battle groups, amphibious forces, or of operating independently and as flagships of surface action groups. Due to their extensive combat capability, these ships have been designated as Battle Force Capable (BFC) units. The cruisers are equipped with *Tomahawk* ASM/LAM giving them additional long range strike mission capability.

Background: Technological advances in the Standard Missile coupled with the AEGIS combat system in *Ticonderoga* class cruisers and the upgrading of older cruisers have increased the AAW capability of surface combatants to pinpoint accuracy from wave-top to zenith. The addition of *Tomahawk* ASM/LAM in the CG-47 class has vastly complicated unit target planning for any potential enemy and returned an offensive strike role to the surface forces that seemed to have been lost to air power at Pearl Harbor.

The *California*-class nuclear-powered guided-missile cruisers were inactivated at the end of Fiscal Year 1998.

GENERAL CHARACTERISTICS, *TICONDEROGA* CLASS

Builders:
Ingalls Shipbuilding: CG 47-50, CG 52-57, 59,62, 65-66, 68-69, 71-73
Bath Iron Works: CG-51,58,60-61,63-64,67,70.
Power Plant: 4 General Electric LM 2500 gas turbine engines; 2 shafts, 80,000 shaft horsepower total.
Length: 567 feet (172.82 meters)
Beam: 55 feet (16.76 meters)
Displacement: 9,600 long tons (9,754.06 metric tons) full load
Speed: 30+ knots (34.52+mph, 55.55+ kph)
Aircraft: Two SH-2 *Seasprite* (LAMPS) in CG 47-48; Two SH-60 *Sea Hawk* (LAMPS III)
Cost: About $1 billion each

SHIPS:

Homeport, Norfolk, VA.
USS Leyte Gulf (CG 55)
USS San Jacinto (CG 56)
USS Philippine Sea (CG 58)
USS Normandy (CG 60)
USS Monterey (CG 61)
USS Gettysburg (CG 64)
USS Anzio (CG 68)
USS Cape St. George (CG 71)
USS Vella Gulf (CG 72)
Homeport, San Diego, CA.
USS Valley Forge (CG 50)
USS Bunker Hill (CG 52)
USS Antietam (CG 54)
USS Lake Champlain (CG 57)
USS Princeton (CG 59)

USS Cowpens (CG 63)
USS Shiloh (CG 67)
Homeport: Pascagoula, MS.
USS Ticonderoga (CG 47)
USS Yorktown (CG 48)
USS Thomas S. Gates (CG 51)
Homeport: Yokosuka, Japan
USS Vincennes (CG 49),
USS Mobile Bay (CG 53),
USS Chancellorsville (CG 62)
Homeport Mayport, FL.
USS Hue City (CG 66)
USS Vicksburg (CG 69)
Homeport: Pearl Harbor, HI.
USS Chosin (CG 65)
USS Lake Erie (CG 70)
USS Port Royal (CG 73)

Crew: 24 Officers, 340 Enlisted

Armament: MK26 missile launcher (CG 47 thru CG 51) or MK41 vertical launching system (CG 52 thru CG 73) *Standard* Missile (MR); Anti-Submarine Rocket (ASROC); *Tomahawk* ASM/LAM; Six MK-46 torpedoes (from two triple mounts); Two MK 45 5-inch/54 caliber lightweight guns; Two *Phalanx* close-in-weapons systems
Date Deployed: 22 January 1983 *(USS Ticonderoga)*

DESTROYERS – DD, DDG

These fast warships help safeguard larger ships in a fleet or battle group.

Features: Destroyers and guided missile destroyers operate in support of carrier battle groups, surface action groups, amphibious groups and replenishment groups. Destroyers primarily perform anti-submarine warfare duty while guided missile destroyers are multi-mission (ASW, anti-air and anti-surface warfare) surface combatants. The addition of the Mk-41 Vertical Launch System or *Tomahawk* Armored Box Launchers (ABLs) to many *Spruance*-class destroyers has greatly expanded the role of the destroyer in strike warfare.

Background: Technological advances have improved the capability of modern destroyers culminating in the *Arleigh Burke* (DDG 51) class. Named for the Navy's most famous destroyer squadron combat commander and three-time Chief of Naval Operations, the *Arleigh Burke* was commissioned July 4, 1991 and was the most powerful surface com-

batant ever put to sea. Like the larger *Ticonderoga* class cruisers, DDG-51's combat systems center around the Aegis combat system and the *SPY-lD*, multi-function phased array radar. The combination of *Aegis*, the Vertical Launching System, an advanced anti-submarine warfare system, advanced anti-aircraft missiles and *Tomahawk* ASM/LAM, the *Burke* class continues the revolution at sea.

Designed for survivability, DDG-51 incorporates all-steel construction and many damage control features resulting from lessons learned during the Falkland Islands War and from the accidental attack on *USS Stark*. Like most modern U.S. surface combatants, DDG-51 utilizes gas turbine propulsion. These ships replaced the older *Charles F. Adams* and *Farragut*-class guided missile destroyers.

The *Spruance* class destroyers, the first large U.S. Navy warships to employ gas turbine engines as their main propulsion system, are undergoing extensive modernizing. The upgrade program includes addition of vertical launchers for advanced missiles on 24 ships of this class, in addition to an advanced ASW system and upgrading of its helicopter capability. *Spruance* class destroyers are expected to remain a major part of the Navy's surface combatant force into the 21st century.

GENERAL CHARACTERISTICS, *ARLEIGH BURKE* CLASS

Builders: Bath Iron Works, Ingalls Shipbuilding
Power Plant: Four General Electric LM 2500-30 gas turbines; two shafts, 100,000 total shaft horsepower.
Length: 466 feet (142 meters)
Beam: 59 feet (18 meters)
Displacement: 8,300 tons (8,433.2 metric tons) full load
Speed: in excess of 30 knots
Aircraft: None. LAMPS III electronics installed on landing deck for coordinated DDG 51/helo ASW operations

SHIPS:

Homeport: Mayport, Fla.
USS Carney (DDG 64),
USS The Sullivans (DDG 68)
Homeport: Norfolk, VA
USS Arleigh Burke (DDG 51)
USS Barry (DDG 52)

USS Stout (DDG 55)
USS Mitscher (DDG 57)
USS Laboon (DDG 58)
USS Ramage (DDG 61),
USS Gonzalez (DDG 66)
USS Cole (DDG 67)
USS Ross (DDG 71)
USS Mahan (DDG 72)
USS McFaul (DDG 74)
USS Donald Cook (DDG 75)
USS Porter (DDG 78)
Homeport: Pearl Harbor, HI
USS Russell (DDG 59)
USS Paul Hamilton (DDG 60)
USS Hopper (DDG 70)
USS O'Kane (DDG 77)
Homeport: San Diego, CA.
USS John Paul Jones (DDG 53)
USS Fitzgerald (DDG 62)
USS Stethem (DDG 63)
USS Benfold (DDG 65)
USS Milius (DDG 69)
USS Decatur (DDG 73)
USS Higgins (DDG 76)
Homeport :Yokosuka, Japan
USS Curtis Wilbur (DDG 54)
USS John S. McCain (DDG 56)
Under construction:
Oscar Austin (DDG 79) Roosevelt (DDG 80)
Winston S. Churchill (DDG 81)
Lassen (DDG 82)
Howard (DDG 83)
Bulkeley (DDG 84)
McCampbell (DDG 85)
Shoup (DDG 86)
Mason (DDG 87)
Preble (DDG 88)
Mustin (DDG 89)
Chafee (DDG 90)

Crew: 23 officers, 300 enlisted

Armament: *Standard* missile; *Harpoon*; Tomahawk ASM/LAM; six Mk-46 torpedoes(from two triple tube mounts); one 5"/54 caliber Mk-45 (lightweight gun); two 20mm *Phalanx* CIWS

Date Deployed: July 4, 1991 *(USS Arleigh Burke)*

GENERAL CHARACTERISTICS, *SPRUANCE* CLASS

Builder: Ingalls Shipbuilding
Power plant: Four General Electric LM 2500 gas turbines, two shafts, 80,000 shaft horsepower
Length: 563 feet (171.6 meters)
Beam: 55 feet (16.8 meters)
Displacement: 9,100 tons (9,246.04

metric tons) full load
Speed: in excess of 30 knots
Aircraft: Two SH-60 *Seahawk* LAMPS III helicopters

SHIPS:

Homeport: Everett, WA.
USS Paul F. Foster (DD 964)
USS David R. Ray (DD 971)
USS Fife (DD 991)
Homeport: Mayport, FL.
USS Spruance (DD 963)
USS John Hancock (DD 981)
USS O'Bannon (DD 987)
Homeport: Norfolk, VA.
USS Arthur W. Radford (DD 968)
USS Peterson (DD 969)
USS Caron (DD 970)
USS Briscoe (DD 977)
USS Stump (DD 978)
USS Thorn (DD 988)
USS Deyo (DD 989)
USS Moosbrugger (DD 980)
USS Nicholson (DD 982)
USS Hayler (DD 997)
Homeport: Pearl Harbor, HI.
USS Fletcher (DD 992)
Homeport: San Diego, CA.
USS Kinkaid (DD 965)
USS Hewitt (DD 966)
USS Elliot (DD 967)
USS Oldendorf (DD 972)
USS John Young (DD 973)
Homeport: Yokosuka, Japan
USS O'Brien (DD 975)
USS Cushing (DD 985)

Crew: 30 officers, 352 enlisted
Armament: 8 *Harpoon* (from 2 quad launchers), *Tomahawk* ASM/LAM, VLS or ABL; ASROC; six Mk-46 torpedoes (from 2 triple tube mounts); two 5"/54 caliber Mk-45 (lightweight gun); two 20mm *Phalanx* CIWS *Kidd* class only: *Standard* missiles; NATO *Sea Sparrow* point defense AAW missiles
Date Deployed:
Sept. 20, 1975 *(USS Spruance)*

DOCK LANDING SHIP - LSD

Dock Landing Ships support amphibious operations including landings via Landing Craft Air Cushion (LCAC), conventional landing craft and helicopters, onto hostile shores.

Background: These ships transport and launch amphibious craft and vehicles with their crews and embarked person-

nel in amphibious assault operations. LSD-41 was designed specifically to operate LCAC vessels. It has the largest capacity for these landing craft (four) of any U.S. Navy amphibious platform. It will also provide docking and repair services for LCACs and for conventional landing craft.

In 1987, the Navy requested $324.2 million to fund one LSD-41 (Cargo Variant). The ship differs from the original LSD-41 by reducing its number of LCACs to two in favor of additional, cargo capacity.

GENERAL CHARACTERISTICS, *HARPERS FERRY* CLASS

Builders: Avondale Industries Inc., New Orleans, La.
Power Plant: Four Colt Industries , 16 Cylinder Diesels, two shafts, 33,000 shaft horsepower
Length: 609 feet (185.62 meters)
Beam: 84 feet (25.60 meters)
Displacement: 16,708 long tons (16,976.13 metric tons) full load
Speed: 20+ knots (23.02+ miles per hour, 37.05+ kph)
Landing Craft: Two Landing Craft, Air Cushion

SHIPS:

Homeport: Little Creek, VA.
USS Carter Hall (LSD-50)
USS Oak Hill (LSD-51)
Homeport: San Diego, CA.
USS Harpers Ferry (LSD 49)
USS Pearl Harbor (LSD-52)

Crew: Ships Company: 22 officers, 397 enlisted; Marine Detachment: 402 plus 102 surge
Armament: Two 25mm MK 38 Machine Guns, Two 20mm Phalanx CIWS mounts and Six .50 cal. machine guns
Date Deployed: 7 January 1995 (USS *Harpers Ferry*)

GENERAL CHARACTERISTICS, *WHIDBEY ISLAND* CLASS

Builders:
Lockheed Shipbuilding, Seattle, Wa. - LSD-41, 43
Arondale Shipyards, New Orleans , La. - LSD 44-LSD 48
Power Plant: Four Colt Industries , 16 Cylinder Diesels, two shafts, 33,000 shaft horsepower
Length: 609 feet (185.62 meters)
Beam: 84 feet (28.65 meters)

Displacement: 15,939 long tons (16,194.79 metric tons) full load
Speed: 20+ knots (23.5+ miles per hour, 37.05 kph)
Landing Craft: Four Landing Craft, Air Cushion

SHIPS:

Homeport: Little Creek,VA.
USS Whidbey Island (LSD-41)
USS Gunston Hall (LSD-44)
USS Tortuga (LSD-46)
USS Ashland (LSD-48)
Homeport: San Diego, CA.
USS Comstock (LSD-45)
USS Rushmore (LSD-47)
Homeport: Sasebo, Japan
USS Germantown (LSD-42),
USS Fort McHenry (LSD-43)

Crew: Ships Company: 22 officers, 391 enlisted; Marine Detachment: 402 plus 102 surge
Armament: Two 25mm MK 38 Machine Guns; Two 20mm *Phalanx* CIWS mounts and Six .50 cal. machine guns
Date Deployed: Feb. 9, 1985 (USS *Whidbey Island*)

GENERAL CHARACTERISTICS, *ANCHORAGE* CLASS

Builders:
Ingalls Shipbuilding, Pascagoula, Miss.- LSD-36
General Dynamics, Quincy, Mass. - LSD37- LSD40
Power Plant: Two 600 psi boilers, two geared steam turbines, two shafts, 24,000 total shaft horsepower
Length: 553 feet (168.55 meters)
Beam: 85 feet (25.91 meters)
Displacement: 14,000 long tons (14,224.67 metric tons) full load
Speed: 22 knots (25.32+ miles per hour, 40.75+ km per hour)
Aircraft: None

SHIPS:

Homeport: Little Creek, Va.
USS Portland (LSD-37)
Homeport: San Diego, CA.
USS Anchorage (LSD-36)
USS Mount Vernon (LSD-39)

Crew: Ships Company: 18 officers, 340 enlisted; Marine Detachment: 330
Armament: Four 3-inch/50 cal. twin barrel guns; Two 25mm MK 38 Machine Guns; and two 20mm

Phalanx CIWS
Date Deployed: March 15, 1969

FAST COMBAT SUPPORT SHIPS - AOE

High-speed vessel, designed as oiler, ammunition and supply ship.

Features: The fast combat support ship (AOE) is the Navy's largest combat logistics ship. The AOE has the speed and armament to keep up with the carrier battle groups. It rapidly replenishes Navy task forces and can carry more than 177,000 barrels of oil, 2,150 tons of ammunition, 500 tons of dry stores and 250 tons of refrigerated stores. It receives petroleum products, ammunition and stores from shuttle ships and redistributes these items simultaneously to carrier battle group ships. This reduces the vulnerability of serviced ships by reducing alongside time. Congress appropriated the funds for the lead ship of the AOE 6 (*Supply* class) in 1987.

GENERAL CHARACTERISTICS, *SUPPLY* CLASS

Builders: National Steel and Shipbuilding Co., San Diego, Ca.
Power Plant: Four GE LM2500 gas-turbines; 2 shafts; 105,000 hp
Length: 754 feet (229.82 meters)
Beam: 107 feet (32.61 meters)
Displacement: 48,800 long tons (49,583.15 metric tons) full load
Speed: 25 knots (28.77+ miles per hour, 46.30 km per hour)
Aircraft: Three CH-46E *Sea Knight* helicopters

Ships:

Homeport: Bremerton, WA.
USS Rainer (AOE-7)
USS Bridge (AOE-10)
Homeport: Earle, N.J.
USS Supply (AOE-6)
USS Arctic (AOE-8)
.
Crew: 40 officers, 627 enlisted
Armament: NATO Sea *Sparrow* missiles, two *Phalanx* close-in weapons systems, two 25mm machine guns
Date Deployed: February 26, 1994 - USS Supply (AOE-6)

GENERAL CHARACTERISTICS, *SACRAMENTO* CLASS

Builders:
AOE 1, 3, 4, Puget Sound Naval Shipyard
AOE 2, New York Shipbuilding

Unit Cost: $458-568 million
Power Plant: Four boilers, geared turbines, two shafts, 100,000 shaft horsepower
Length: 793 feet (241.71 meters)
Beam: 107 feet (32.61 meters)
Displacement: 53,000 long tons (53,850.55 metric tons) full load
Speed: 26+ knots (29.92+ miles, 48.15 km, per hour)
Aircraft: Two CH-46E *Sea Knight* helicopters

SHIPS:

Homeport: Bremerton, WA.
USS Sacramento (AOE-1)
USS Camden (AOE-2)
Homeport: Earle, NJ.
USS Seattle (AOE-3)
USS Detroit (AOE-4)

Crew: 24 officers, 576 enlisted
Armament: NATO *Sea Sparrow* missiles, two *Phalanx* close-in weapons systems.
Date Deployed: March 14, 1964 - *USS Sacramento* (AOE-1)

FLEET OCEAN TUGS - T-ATF

Seven ocean-going tugs are operated by Military Sealift Command and provide the U.S. Navy with towing service, and when augmented by Navy divers, assist in the recovery of downed aircraft and ships.

Features: Each vessel is equipped with 10 ton capacity crane and a bollard pull of at least 54 tons. A deck grid is fitted aft which contains 1 inch bolt receptacles spaced 24 inches apart. This allows for the bolting down of a wide variety of portable equipment. There are two GPH fire pumps supplying three fire monitors with up to 2,200 gallons of foam per minute. A deep module can be embarked to support naval salvage teams.

Background: Fleet tugs are used to tow ships, barges and targets for gunnery exercises. They are also used as platforms for salvage and diving work, as participants in naval exercises, to conduct search and rescue missions, to aid in the clean up of oil spills and ocean accidents, and to provide fire fighting assistance. *USNS Apache* (T-ATF 172) is the last of the *Powhatan* class of ocean tugs delivered to the Navy in 1981.

GENERAL CHARACTERISTICS: *POWHATAN* CLASS

Builder: Marinette Marine Corporation, Marinette, Wisc
Power Plant: 2 GM EMD 20-645F7B diesels; 5.73 MW sustained; 2 shafts; Kort nozzles (except on *Powhatan* and one other); cp props; bow thruster; 300 hp (224 kW)
Length: 226 feet (68.88 meters)
Beam: 42 feet (12.80 meters)
Displacement: 2,260 long tons (2,296.27 metric tons) full load
Speed: 14.5 knots (16.69 mph, 26.86)

SHIPS: No home ports assigned

USNS Powhatan (T-ATF 166)
USNS Narragansett (T-ATF 167)
USNS Catawba (T-ATF 168)
USNS Navajo (T-ATF 169)
USNS Mohawk (T-ATF 170)
USNS Sioux (T-ATF 171)
USNS Apache (T-ATF 172)

Crew: 16 civilians and 4 naval communications technicians

FRIGATES - FFG

Frigates fulfill a Protection of Shipping (POS) mission as Anti-Submarine Warfare (ASW) combatants for amphibious expeditionary forces, underway replenishment groups and merchant convoys.

Background: The guided missile frigates (FFG) bring an anti-air warfare (AAW) capability to the frigate mission, but they have some limitations. Designed as cost efficient surface combatants, they lack the multi-mission capability necessary for modern surface combatants faced with multiple, high-technology threats. They also offer limited capacity for growth. Despite this, the FFG-7 class is a robust platform, capable of withstanding considerable damage. This "toughness" was aptly demonstrated when *USS Samuel B.*

Roberts struck a mine and *USS Stark* was hit by two Exocet cruise missiles. In both cases the ships survived, were repaired and returned to the fleet. *USS Stark* was recently decommissioned in May 1999.

The Surface Combatant Force Requirement Study does not define any need for a single mission ship such as the frigate and there are no frigates planned in the Navy's five-year ship-building plan.

GENERAL CHARACTERISTICS, *OLIVER HAZARD PERRY* CLASS

Builders: Bath Iron Works: FFG 8, 11, 13, 15, 29, 32, 36, 39, 42, 45, 47, 49, 50, 53, 55, 56, 58, 59.
Todd Shipyards, Seattle: FFG 28, 31, 37, 40, 48, 52.
Todd Shipyards, San Pedro, Calif.: FFG 9, 12, 14, 19, 23, 30, 33, 38, 41, 43, 46, 51, 54, 57, 60, 61.
Power Plant: Two General Electric LM 2500 gas turbine engines; 1 shaft, 41,000 shaft horsepower total.
Length: 445 feet (133.64 meters); 453 feet (138.07 meters) with *LAMPS III* modification.
Beam: 45 feet (13.72 meters)
Displacement: 4,100 long tons (4,165.80 metric tons) full load
Speed: 29 plus knots (33.37+ miles, 54.28+ km, per hour)
Aircraft:
Two SH-60 (*LAMPS III*) in FFG 8, 28, 29, 32, 33, 36-61
One SH-2F (*Lamps* Mk-I) in FFG 9-19, 30, 31.

SHIPS:

Homeport: Everett, WA.
USS Ford (FFG-54)
USS Rodney M. Davis (FFG-60)
USS Ingraham (FFG-61)
Homport: Mayport, FL.
USS McInerney (FFG-8)
USS Samuel Eliot Morison (FFG-13)
USS Boone (FFG-28)
USS Underwood (FFG-36)
USS Doyle (FFG-39)
USS Klakring (FFG-42)
USS Robert G. Bradley (FFG-49).
USS Taylor (FFG-50)
USS DeWert (FFG-45)
Home Port: Norfolk, VA.
USS Clark (FFG-11)
USS Estocin (FFG-15)
USS Halyburton (FFG-40)

USS Nicholas (FFG-47)
USS Carr (FFG-52)
USS Hawes (FFG-53)
USS Elrod (FFG-55)
USS Simpson (FFG-56)
USS Samuel B. Roberts (FFG-58)
USS Kauffman (FFG-59)
Homeport: Pascagoula, MS.
USS Stephen W. Groves (FFG-29)
USS John L. Hall (FFG-32)
Homeport: Pearl Harbor, HI
USS Crommelin (FFG-37)
USS Reuben James (FFG-57)
Homeport: San Diego, CA.
USS Wadsworth (FFG-9)
USS George Philip (FFG-12)
USS Sides (FFG-14)
USS John A. Moore (FFG-19)
USS Jarrett (FFG-33)
USS Curts (FFG-38)
USS McClusky (FFG-41)
USS Thach (FFG-43)
USS Rentz (FFG-46)
Homeport: Yokosuka, Japan
USS Vandegrift (FFG-48)
USS Gary (FFG-51)

Crew: 13 Officers, 287 Enlisted
Armament: Standard Missile (MR); Harpoon (from *Standard* Missile Launcher); Six MK-46 torpedoes(from two triple mounts); One 76 mm (3-inch)/62 caliber MK 75 rapid fire gun; One *Phalanx* close-in-weapons system
Date Deployed: 17 December 1977 (*Oliver Hazard Perry*)

HOSPITAL SHIPS - T-AH

Two hospital ships operated by Military Sealift Command are designed to provide emergency, on-site care for U.S. combatant forces deployed in war or other operations.

Features: *USNS Mercy* (T-AH 19) and *USNS Comfort* (T-AH 20) each contain 12 fully-equipped operating rooms, a 1,000 bed hospital facility, radiological services, medical laboratory, a pharmacy, an optometry lab, a cat scan and two oxygen producing plants. Both vessels have a helicopter deck capable of landing large military helicopters, as well as side ports to take on patients at sea.

Background: Both hospital ships are converted *San Clemente*-class super tankers. *Mercy* was delivered in 1986 and *Comfort* in 1987. Normally, the ships are kept in a reduced operating status in Baltimore, Md., and San Diego, Calif., by a small crew of civilian mariners and active duty Navy medical and support personnel. Each ship can be fully activated and crewed within five days. Mercy went to the Philippines in 1987 for a humanitarian mission. Both ships were used during *Operation Desert Shield/Storm. Comfort* twice operated during 1994 — once for *Operation Sea Signal's* Cuban/Haitian migrant interdiction operations, and a second time supporting U.S. forces and agencies involved in Haiti and *Operation Uphold Democracy.* In 1998, *Comfort* participated in exercise *Baltic Challenge '98*, a multinational exercise involving 11 European nations and the United States to improve cooperation in peace support operations

GENERAL CHARACTERISTCS: *MERCY* CLASS

Conversion: National Steel and Shipbuilding Co., San Diego, Calif.
Power Plant: 2 GE turbines; two boilers; 24,500 hp (18.3MW); one shaft
Length: 894 feet (272.6 meters)
Beam: 105.6 feet (32.2 meters)
Displacement: 69,360 tons (70,473.10 metric tons) full load
Speed: 17.5 knots (20.13 mph)
Aircraft: Helicopter platform only

SHIPS: No home ports assigned

USNS Mercy (T-AH 19)
USNS Comfort (T-AH 20)

Crew: 63 civilian mariners, 956 Naval medical staff, and 258 Naval support staff

LANDING CRAFT, MECHANIZED AND UTILITY - LCM/LCU

Landing craft are used by amphibious forces to transport equipment and troops to the shore.

Features: Landing craft are capable of transporting tracked or wheeled vehicles and troops from amphibious assault ships to beachheads or piers. LCM's feature a bow ramp for onload and offload. LCU's have both

bow and stern ramps for onload/offload at either end.

Background: The use of landing craft in amphibious assault dates from World War II. The craft are carried aboard amphibious assault ships to the objective area.

GENERAL CHARACTERISTICS, LCU 1610, 1627 AND 1646 CLASS

Power Plant: :2- Detroit 12V-71 Diesel engines, twin shaft, 680 hp sustained, Kort nozzles
Length: 134.9 feet (41.12 meters)
Beam: 29 feet (8.84 meters)
Displacement: 200 long tons (203.21 metric tons) light; 375 long tons (381.02 metric tons) full load
Speed: 11 kts (12.66 mph, 20.37 kph)
Range: 1200 miles at 8 knots
Capacity: 170 tons
Military Lift: 125 tons of cargo
Crew: 14
Guns: 2- 12.7mm MGs
Radar: Navigation:LN 66 or SPS-53; I band.

GENERAL CHARACTERISTICS, LCM 8 TYPE

Power Plant:2- Detroit 12V-71 Diesel engines; 680hp sustained; twin shafts
Length: 73.7 feet (22.46 meters)
Beam: 21 feet (6.4 meters)
Displacement: 105 long tons (106.69 metric tons) full load
Speed: 12 kts (13.81 mph, 22.22 kph)
Range: 190 miles at 9kts full load
Capacity: 180 tons
Military lift: 1- M48 or 1- M60 tank or 200 troops
Crew: 5

GENERAL CHARACTERISTICS, LCM 6 TYPE

Power Plant: 2- Detroit 6-71 Diesel engines; 348 hp sustained; twin shaft, or 2- Detroit 8V-71 Diesel engines; 460 hp sustained; twin shaft
Length: 56.2 feet (17.13 meters)
Beam: 14 feet (4.27 meters)
Displacement: 64 long tons (65.03 metric tons) full load
Speed: 9 kts (10.36 mph, 16.67 kph)
Range:130 miles at 9 kts
Military lift: 34 tons or 80 troops
Crew: 5

LANDING CRAFT, AIR CUSHIONED (LCAC)

Air cushion craft for transporting, ship-to-shore and across the beach, personnel, weapons, equipment, and cargo of the assault elements of the Marine Air-Ground Task Force.

Features: The landing craft air cushion (LCAC) is a high-speed, over-the-beach fully amphibious landing craft capable of carrying a 60-75 ton payload. It is used to transport weapons systems, equipment, cargo and personnel from ship to shore and across the beach. The advantages of air-cushion landing craft are numerous. They can carry heavy payloads, such as an M-1 tank, at high speeds. Their payload and speed mean more forces reach the shore in a shorter time, with shorter intervals between trips. The air cushion allows this vehicle to reach more than 70 percent of the world's coastline, while conventional landing craft can land at only 15 percent of the coasts.

Background: Thirty-three air-cushion landing craft were authorized and appropriated through FY86. An additional 15 were funded in FY89, 12 more in FY90 and FY91. The remaining 24 were funded in FY92. As of December 1995, 82 LCACs had been delivered to the Navy.

GENERAL CHARACTERISTICS

Class: LCAC-1
Builder: Textron Marine and Land Systems/Avondale Gulfport Marine
Power Plant: 4- Avco-Lycoming TF-40B gas turbines (2 for propulsion/2 for lift); 16,000 hp sustained; 2- shrouded reversible pitch airscrews; 4- double-entry fans, centrifugal or mixed flow (lift)
Length: 87 feet 11 inches (26.80 meters)
Beam: 47 feet (14.33 meters)
Displacement: 87.2 long tons (88.60 metric tons) light; 170-182 long tons (172.73 - 184.92 metric tons) full load
Range: 200 miles at 40 kts with payload / 300 miles at 35 kts with payload
Speed: 40+ knots (46+ mph; 74.08 kph) with full load
Load Capacity: 60 tons / 75 ton overload
Military lift: 24 troops or 1 MBT

Crew: Five
Armament: 2 - 12.7mm MGs. Gun mounts will support: M-2HB .50 cal machine gun; Mk-19 Mod3 40mm grenade launcher; M-60 machine gun
Radars: Navigation: Marconi LN 66; I band
Date Deployed: 1982

MARK V SPECIAL OPERATIONS CRAFT

The Mark V is used to carry Special Operations Forces (SOF), primarily SEAL combat swimmers, into and out of operations where the threat to these forces is considered to be low to medium. They also support limited coastal patrol and interruption of enemy activities.

Background: The MARK V Special Operations Craft (SOC) is the newest, versatile, high performance combatant craft introduced into the Naval Special Warfare (NSW) Special Boat Squadron (SBR) inventory to improve maritime special operations capabilities.

MARK Vs are organized into detachments comprised of two boats, crews and a deployment support package mounted on cargo transporters. The detachment can be delivered in-theater rapidly by two C-5 aircraft, by a well or flight deck equipped surface ships and, if appropriate, under their own power. The detachment can be deployable within 48 hours of notification and ready for operations within 24 hours of arrival at a forward operating base. They can operate from shore facilities, from well-deck equipped ships or from ships with appropriate crane and deck space capabilities.

The MARK Vs are a result of a streamlined acquisition effort managed by the United States Special Operations Command (USSOCOM) Special Operations Acquisition Executive (SOAE). From the awarding of the contract to actual possession of the first boat took only 18 months.

GENERAL CHARACTERISTICS:

Length: 82 feet (24.99 meters)
Beam: 17 feet 6 inches (5.33 meters)

Weight: 57 long tons (57.91 metric tons)
Speed: 50 knots (57.54+ mph, 92.60 kph)

MINE COUNTERMEASURES SHIP – MCS

Dedicated command, control and support ship for mine countermeasures operations. To learn more about Mine Warfare visit their command's web site.
Background: *Operations Desert Shield* and *Desert Storm* identified the need for a dedicated command, control and support ship to support mine countermeasures operations. The contract to convert *Inchon* was awarded in November 1994 to Ingalls Shipbuilding, Inc., Pascagoula, Miss.

Features: *USS Inchon* was converted from an amphibious assault ship with major changes made to the Command, Control, Communica-tions, Computers and Intelligence (C4I) system including upgrades to the close-in weapons system (*Phalanx*) and various radars. The ship supports an embarked composite helicopter squadron of eight CH-53E and two SAR/spotter helicopters, and provides alongside support and services for up to four MCM/MHC ships. It can support and accommodate four Explosive Ordnance Disposal (EOD) groups with assigned equipment. Additionally it provides C4I facilities for the MCM group commander. New repair facilities and upgrades to older one were also added, giving the MSC 12 the ability to accomplish whatever repairs are necessary to weapons, LCACs, aircraft, etc., in any theater of operation.

GENERAL CHARACTERISTICS, *INCHON* CLASS

Builders: Ingalls Shipbuilding, Pascagoula, Miss.
Power Plant: 600-pound steam plant, one shaft, 22,000 shaft horsepower
Length: 602 feet (183.49 meters)
Beam: 84 feet (25.6 meters)
Displacement: 19,600 long tons (19,914.54 metric tons) full load
Speed: 21 knots (24.17 miles per hour)

Aircraft:
Two UH-46D *Sea Knight* helicopters and eight MH-53E *Sea Stallion* helicopters.

Homeport: Ingleside, Tex
Ship: USS Inchon (MCS 12),

Crew: 122 officers; 1,321 enlisted
Armament: Four .50 caliber machine guns; four 25mm MK 38 machine guns; two *Phalanx* CIWS; Stingers.

MINE COUNTERMEASURES SHIPS - MCM

Ships designed to clear mines from vital waterways.

Background: In the early 1980s, the U.S. Navy began development of a new mine countermeasures (MCM) force, which included two new classes of ships and mine sweeping helicopters. The vital importance of a state-of-the-art mine countermeasures force was strongly underscored in the Persian Gulf during the eight years of the Iran-Iraq war, and in *Operations Desert Shield* and *Desert Storm* in 1990 and 1991 when the *Avenger* (MCM 1) and *Guardian* (MCM 5) ships conducted MCM operations. To learn more about Mine Warfare visit their command's web site.
Avenger class ships are designed as mine hunter-killers capable of finding, classifying and destroying moored and bottom mines. The last three MCM ships were purchased in 1990, bringing the total to 14 fully deployable, ocean-going *Avenger* class ships.

These ships use sonar and video systems, cable cutters and a mine-detonating device that can be released and detonated by remote control. They are also capable of conventional sweeping measures. The ships are of fiberglass sheathed, wooden hull construction. They are the first large mine countermeasures ships built in the United States in nearly 27 years.

Osprey (MHC 51) class ships are also designed as mine hunter-killers. The MHC 51 has a 15-day endurance and depends on a support ship or shore based facilities for re-supply.

GENERAL CHARACTERISTICS, *AVENGER* CLASS

Builders: Peterson Shipbuilders, Sturgeon Bay, Wis.; Marinette Marine, Marinette, Wis.
Power Plant: Four diesels (600 horse-

power each), two shafts with controllable pitch propellers
Length: 224 feet (68.28 meters)
Beam: 39 feet (11.89 meters)
Displacement: 1,312 long tons (1,333.06 metric tons) full load
Speed: 14 knots (16.11 mph, 25.93 kmph)

SHIPS: (All MCM-1 class ships are based in Ingleside, Texas unless noted.)

USS Avenger (MCM 1)
USS Defender (MCM 2)
USS Sentry (MCM 3)
USS Champion (MCM 4)
USS Guardian (MCM 5); **Permanently forward deployed Sasebo, Japan**
USS Devastator (MCM 6)
USS Patriot (MCM 7);
USS Scout (MCM 8)
USS Pioneer (MCM 9)
USS Warrior (MCM 10)
USS Gladiator (MCM 11)
USS Ardent (MCM 12);
Forward deployed Arabian Gulf
USS Dextrous (MCM 13)
USS Chief (MCM 14)

Crew: 8 officers, 76 enlisted
Armament: Mine neutralization system. Two .50 caliber machine guns
Date Deployed: Sept. 12, 1987 (*USS Avenger*)

PATROL COASTAL BOATS - PC

Description: The primary mission of these ships is coastal patrol and interdiction surveillance, an important aspect of littoral operations outlined in the Navy's strategy, *Forward...From the Sea*. These ships also provide full mission support for Navy SEALs and other special operations forces.

Background: The *Cyclone* class ships are assigned to Naval Special Warfare. Of the thirteen ships, nine operate out of the Naval Amphibious Base, Little Creek, Va., and four operate from the Naval Amphibious Base, Coronado, Calif. These ships provide the Naval Special Warfare Command with a fast, reliable platform that can respond to emergent requirements in a low intensity conflict environment.

GENERAL CHARACTERISTICS, *CYCLONE* CLASS

Builders: Bollinger Shipyards, Inc.
Power Plant: Four Paxman diesels; four shafts; 3,350 shaft horsepower
Length: 170 feet (51.82 meters)
Beam: 25 feet (7.62 meters)
Displacement: 331 tons (336.31 metric tons) full load
Speed: 35 knots (40 miles per hour; 65 kilometers/hr.)

SHIPS:

Homeport: Little Creek, VA.
USS Cyclone (PC 1)
USS Tempest (PC 2)
USS Typhoon (PC 5)
USS Sirocco (PC 6)
USS Chinook (PC 9)
USS Firebolt (PC 10)
USS Whirlwind (PC 11)
USS Thunderbolt (PC 12)
USS Shamal (PC 13)
Homeport: San Diego, CA.
USS Hurricane (PC 3)
USS Monsoon (PC 4)
USS Squall (PC 7)
USS Zephyr (PC 8)
Under construction:
Tornado (PC 14)

Crew: Four officers, 24 enlisted personnel; eight Special Forces personnel
Armament: Two 25mm MK 38 machine guns; two .50 caliber machine guns; two MK 19 automatic grenade launchers; six Stinger missiles.

RESCUE AND SALVAGE SHIPS - ARS

Rescue and salvage ships render assistance to disabled ships, provide towing, salvage, diving, firefighting and heavy lift capabilities.

Features: The mission of the rescue and salvage ships is four-fold: to debeach stranded vessels, heavy lift capability from ocean depths, towing of other vessels, and manned diving operations. For rescue missions, these ships are equipped with fire monitors forward and amidships which can deliver either firefighting foam or sea water. The salvage holds of these ships are outfitted with portable equipment to provide assistance to other vessels in dewatering, patching, supply of electrical power and other

essential service required to return a disabled ship to an operating condition.

Background: The U.S. Navy has responsibility for salvaging U.S. government-owned ships and, when it is in the best interests of the United States, privately-owned vessels as well. The rugged construction of these steel-hulled ships, combined with speed and endurance, make these rescue and salvage ships well-suited for rescue/salvage operations of Navy and commercial shipping throughout the world. The versatility of this class of ship adds immeasurably to the capabilities of the U.S. Navy with regard to rendering assistance to those in peril on the high seas.

GENERAL CHARACTERISTICS, *SAFEGUARD* CLASS

Primary Function: Fire fighting, combat salvage, rescue towing, diving
Builders: Peterson Builders
Power Plant: Four Caterpiller 399 Diesels, two shafts, 4,200 horsepower
Length: 255 feet (77.7 meters)
Beam: 51 feet (15.5 meters)
Draft: 16 feet 9 inches (5.11 meters)
Displacement: 3,282 tons (3,334.67 metric tons) full load
Speed: 14 knots (16.1 miles, 25.8 km, per hour)
Endurance: 8,000 miles (12,872 km) at 8 knots (9.2 km/hr)
Salvage capability: 7.5-ton capacity boom forward; 40-ton capacity boom aft
Heavy lift: Capable of a hauling force of 150 tons
Diving Depth: 190 feet (57.9 meters), using air

SHIPS:

Homeport: Little Creek, Va.
USS Grasp (ARS 51)
USS Grapple (ARS 53)
Homeport: Pearl Harbor, HI
USS Safeguard (ARS 50)
USS Salvor (ARS 52)

Crew: 6 officers, 94 enlisted
Armament: Two .50 caliber machine guns; two Mk-38 25mm guns
Date Deployed: August 16, 1985

TANK LANDING SHIPS - LST

Description: Tank landing ships (LST) are used to transport and land tanks, amphibious vehicles and other rolling stock in amphibious assault.

Features: Ships of this class are the first to depart from the bow-door design that characterized the workhorses of World War II. The hull form necessary to attain the 20-knot speeds of contemporary amphibious squadrons would not permit bow doors. Accordingly, these ships off load cargo and vehicles by means of a 112-foot ramp over their bow. A stern gate allows off-loading of amphibious vehicles directly into the water. The two ships of this class, now assigned to the Naval Reserve Forces, are the only of this 20-ship class of LSTs remaining in the fleet.

GENERAL CHARACTERISTICS, *NEWPORT* CLASS

Builders: National Steel and Shipbuilding
Power plant: Six diesels, two shafts, 16,000 brake horsepower
Length: 522 feet (159.11 meters)
Beam: 69 feet (21.03 meters)
Displacement: 8,450 long tons (8,585.61 metric tons) full load
Speed: 20 knots (23.02 miles, 37.05 km, per hour)

SHIPS:

Home Port: Little Creek, VA.
USS La Moure County (LST-1194),
Home Port: Pearl Harbor, HI
USS Frederick (LST-1184),

Crew: 13 officers, 244 enlisted
Armament: One 20 mm Phalanx CIWS mount; two 25 mm MK 38 machine guns
Date Deployed: June 7, 1969 (*USS Newport*)

UNDERWAY REPLENISHMENT OILERS - T-AO

Description: Thirteen underway replenishment oilers are operated by Military Sealift Command and provide underway replenishment of fuel to U.S. Navy ships at sea and jet fuel for aircraft assigned to aircraft carriers. Three of the newest MSC underway replenishment oilers have double hulls.

Features: There are stations on both sides of each ship for underway replenishment of fuel and stores.

Background: Fitted with integrated electrical auxiliary propulsion, the delivery of *USNS Patuxent* (T-ATF 201), *USNS Rappahannock* (T-ATF 204) and *USNS Laramie* (T-ATF 203) was delayed by the decision to fit double hulls to meet the requirements of the Oil Pollution Act of 1990. This modification increased construction time from 32 to 42 months and reduced cargo capacity by 17 percent, although this can be restored in an emergency. Hull separation is 1.83 m at the sides and 1.98 m on the bottom. *USNS Henry J. Kaiser* (T-AO 187) has become part of the MSC Prepositioning Program at Diego Garcia, carrying aviation fuel.

GENERAL CHARACTERISTICS: *HENRY J. KAISER* CLASS

Builder: Avondale Shipyards, Inc., New Orleans, La.
Power Plant: 2 Colt-Pielstick 10 PC4.2 V 570 diesels; 34,442 hp(m) (24.3MW) sustained; 2 shafts; cp props
Length: 677.5 feet (206.50 meters)
Beam: 97.5 feet (29.72 meters)
Displacement: 40,700 long tons (41,353.16 metric ton); 42,000 long tons (42,674.02 metric tons) [T-AO 201, 203-204] full load
Capactiy: 180,000; 159,000 [T-AO 201, 203-204] barrels of fuel oil or aviation fuel
Speed: 20 knots (23 mph, 37.05 kph)

SHIPS: No homeports assigned

USNS Henry J. Kaiser (TAO 187)
USNS Walter S. Diehl (T-AO 193)
USNS Ericsson (T-AO 194)
USNS Leroy Grumman (T-AO 195)
USNS Kanawha (T-AO 196)
USNS Pecos (T-AO 197)
USNS Big Horn (T-AO 198)
USNS Tippecanoe (T-AO 199)
USNS Guadalupe (T-AO 200)
USNS Patuxent (T-AO 201)
USNS Yukon (T-AO 202)
USNS Laramie (T-AO 203)
USNS Rappahannock (T-AO 204)

Crew: 82 civilian crew (18 officers); 21 Navy (1 officer) plus 21 spare
Aircraft: Helicopter platform only

Litton
Ship Systems

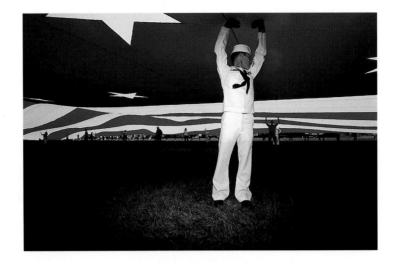

sippican, inc.

United Defense

Patrons: MarineSafety International - Whitney, Bradley and Brown, Inc.

Our thanks to the Surface Navy Association and the corporations whose generous grants helped to create this documentary book. Our warmest thanks and appreciation to the many fine people of America's Surface Fleet and Marine Corps, some of whom are pictured in this book.

A very special thank you to the many great people who helped facilitate this project:
RADM William A. Retz, USN(Ret), along with VADM Douglas J. Katz, USN (Ret), VADM Joseph Metcalf III, USN (Ret), and CAPT Kenneth A. Jarvis USNR. All helped tremendously with their insights and positive critiques.

Lt. Bob Mehal and all the people who serve at the Navy Office of Information (CHINFO). All the Public Affairs Officers in the Navy and Marine Corps whom without their extra efforts this project would have been impossible.

Fred Rainbow, editor and Dave Hoefling, photo editor of Proceedings Magazine for their unselfish support and advice in helping to polish this project.

And finally, a thank you to my wife Judy who maintained the business and home front while I was traveling and to my son Stephen who endured all the missed ball games, birthdays and holidays.